MOUNT MARY
Milwaukee, W   W9-AEN-456

The Half-Parent

By the same author

BEYOND BABEL
NEW DIRECTIONS IN COMMUNICATIONS

MOUNT MARY COLLEGE LIBRARY
Milwaukee, Wisconsin 53222

The Half-Parent

Living with Other People's Children

Brenda Maddox

Preface by Mel Krantzler
Author of CREATIVE DIVORCE

M. EVANS AND COMPANY, INC.
New York, New York 10017

76-1183

M. Evans and Company titles are distributed in
the United States by the J. B. Lippincott Company,
East Washington Square, Philadelphia, Pa. 19105;
and in Canada by McClelland & Stewart Ltd.,
25 Hoilinger Road, Toronto M4B 3G2, Ontario

LIBRARY OF CONGRESS CATALOGING IN PUBLICATION DATA
Maddox, Brenda.
    The half-parent.
    1. Children—Management. 2. Stepparents. 3. Step-
children. I. Title.
HQ769.M235 1975   301.42'7   75-17780
ISBN 0-87131-182-8

Copyright © 1975 by Brenda Maddox
All rights reserved under International and
Pan-American Copyright Conventions

Design by Joel Schick

Manufactured in the United States of America

9 8 7 6 5 4 3 2 1

301.427
M26

Contents

FOR MY FAMILY

Preface

When I remarried two years ago, I found I had become a member of a vast and neglected group in our society known as stepparents. Each year well over half a million adults swell our ranks, yet since we are socially invisible (no one celebrates a "Stepparents' Day" each year) our special problems have been ignored.

Problems, perplexities, dilemmas, and tensions, there are aplenty. And they stem from our new stepparenting role which most of us have been totally unprepared to assume effectively. How to deal with the children of our new spouse? What are the standards of conduct and behavior deemed appropriate to this new relationship? Do we see these children as enhancers, or subverters, of our new marriage? And how do they view us? What have been the typical experiences of other stepparents? Where can we find the common sense suggestions that can help us improve our relationship with our stepchildren?

Until Brenda Maddox wrote *The Half-Parent*, these questions only had their own echo for an answer. *The Half-Parent* is the first popular, broadly comprehensive book about stepparenting that has been written, and readers will find the answers to such questions in its pages. Mrs. Maddox, a stepparent herself, writes compassionately and wisely about all aspects of stepparenting, investing each of her chapters with an authority derived from her own lived experience. One of the book's highlights is the moving, unvarnished story she tells about her own personal life as a stepparent.

The Half-Parent is a candid, thoroughly honest book that does not gloss over the very complex, difficult, and dark sides of stepparenting. This forthrightness reinforces the power of her thesis that stepparenting can be a growth-enhancing experience for all the members of the new family constellation.

In my work as a divorce adjustment counselor I have been searching for quite some time for a book on stepparenting I could recommend to the members of my Creative Divorce Seminars. The publication of *The Half-Parent* ends that search. Here is an essential guide for the well-intentioned, yet very much perplexed, present or future stepparent.

MEL KRANTZLER

San Rafael, California

Foreword

This book is an inquiry into stepparenthood. I wrote it for three reasons. First, as you will see, I found being a stepparent much more difficult than being a parent. I wanted to find out why. Second, as a journalist, I like to ask awkward questions. Stepparenthood certainly presents plenty of these. It is a family relationship that has existed wherever children have depended on two parents; it has fascinated storytellers and gossips and dramatists since antiquity, yet the law, psychiatry, and current social etiquette virtually pretend there is no such thing. My third motive, perhaps the irresistible one, was to present the stepparent's point of view. Our ordinary perception of the step-relationship comes through the eyes of the child – not only the stepchild in fairy stories, but in history and literature – Hamlet, Jesus, and Eliza Doolittle are examples. We are all stepchildren, unappreciated, bullied, full of unrecognized potential.

No one identifies with the stepparent. The relationship is so stereotyped that even stepparents themselves are unsure what their real feelings are. They fumble along with mixed emotions of guilt, irritation, duty, affection, and sometimes love. I was fortunate to be able to interview nearly a hundred stepparents for this book. They talked to me candidly, probably because I am a stepmother myself. Many seemed ashamed even to acknowledge problems, for they said almost with one voice, "I knew what I was getting into." But they did not know what they were getting into, as I hope this book will show. Nor could they, for stepparenthood is so vague and so undefined even in law that with the best will in the world stepparents and stepchildren have to invent their relationship as they go along. There are no rules.

It is curious that a family pattern that has a reputation for being troublesome and that affects more and more children every year should be so ignored. The signs of neglect are everywhere. Any bookstore has shelves and shelves devoted to almost every variation of family life – adoption is a particular favorite – but next to nothing on stepparents or stepchildren. The academic world has been equally uninterested. *Psychological Abstracts*, a monthly international listing of research papers in the social and psychological sciences that distinguishes such categories as maternal behavior and parent-child relations, has had hardly a dozen papers on stepparents since 1927. Dr. Benjamin Spock's *Baby and Child Care* offers advice on twins, the fatherless child, the handicapped child, the adopted child, the child of separated parents, and the child of the working mother. If you have a mongoloid child, you can look him up in Spock: "It is wise to make a tentative application early [for a boarding school] because there is usually a waiting list of several years' duration." But if you have a stepchild, there is nothing in this basic book for you.

But stepparenthood demands investigation. For those involved in it, it raises serious questions to which the answers are by no means common knowledge. How does the incest taboo affect relations between stepparents and stepchildren? Why do some stepparents adopt their stepchildren? Should they? Which is easier, stepparenthood through death or through divorce? Can stepparents and stepchildren marry each other? How true is the myth of the cruel stepparent? Why is the myth harsher on stepmothers than on stepfathers? Are stepchildren prone to delinquency? What part do grandparents play in the adjustment between stepparents and stepchildren? Do stepchildren hate the new baby? What about inheritance? What are the financial obligations of a stepparent toward a stepchild? Does the step-relationship last beyond the marriage that created it?

The fact that the step-relationship has been so ignored demands an explanation in itself. Specialists in family behavior tend to shrug. "Nobody has studied it because nobody has studied it," ventured an analyst from the Anna Freud Clinic in London. A doctor who works for the U.S. Federal Government suggested that stepparenthood was simply a small corner of the enormous money-starved field of child development and family interaction. I heard two more satisfying reasons. One is that the relationship stirs up a great deal of pain. A psychoanalyst from Cambridge, Massachusetts, put it this way: "People go into second marriages with enormous hopes. They have failed once, or they have had their marriage broken by death, and they want everything to go right the next time. They idealize the new partner and then they find that they have the partner's children to deal with as well, and the idealization does not extend to the children. Far from it. The hostility aroused by the children jeopardizes the marriage, so they bury it. The feelings aroused by stepchildren, for many people, simply do not bear looking at."

The second reason, offered by an adoption worker, is that stepfamilies are not accessible. There is a formidable respect for the privacy of the family. When a home is broken, doctors, social workers, friends, even the police if necessary, can go in. When a couple want to adopt a child, they open the doors voluntarily and submit to the intrusion of social agencies and the law; they must if they want the outside world to give them a child. But stepfamilies* are the opposite of broken families. They are remade. A break has been healed, the doors are shut, and the world and the stepfamily itself want to believe that it is just another nuclear family out of the pages of Talcott Parsons or the *Ladies' Home Journal*. No wonder that stepparents feel isolated if they do not live happily ever after with their stepchildren.

Once it became known that I had embarked on this project, I found no shortage of stepparents to interview. In fact, I could not get away from them. Introductions came from doctors, social workers, teachers, and friends, and a great many stepparents themselves volunteered. It was quite common to go for an interview with an anthropologist or a specialist in family law and to leave not only with professional information but also with family secrets and with the names and addresses of friends "who might be interested in talking to you." Most of the people interviewed lived in the United States, but many lived in England,

* I define a stepfamily as a household unit, with a married couple at the head, where a child of one or both of the spouses from a previous marriage lives or is a regular visitor.

where my home is now, including some of that vanishing breed, Americans in England. Almost all were white and middle class. Most were still married to the spouse who had made them a stepparent. This does not imply that poor, black, or divorced stepparents are of no interest; however, they are hard to seek out and must be left to others who have greater financial resources than were available to me.

I did not try to interview the stepchildren of the stepparents. To talk with children about complicated emotions, without any professional training to do so, seemed to me foolhardy. Also, it would have spread my inquiry too thin: this is a book about stepparents. My own stepdaughter chided me, "But how do you know they are telling the truth?" I don't. But I think they told the truth about what they were thinking to themselves, and that is what I wanted to convey. I hope I have disguised the identity of those who talked to me, for while I have changed superficial details, I have not fabricated what they said. There are no phony quotes. In passing, I should like to say a word in praise of my sex. Of course I am prejudiced, but I honestly believe that women have a clearer picture of family life than men do. Men tended to generalize: "I was a terrible stepfather." Women gave direct dialogue, supplied the telling detail. If they had thrown a plate, they said what kind of plate it was.

What follows is no handy list of do's and don'ts for successful stepparenthood. What it is, I hope, is a clarification of a complex relationship that no monogamous society has found easy.

There are no footnotes in the text. However, references to the specific texts quoted as well as to the general background material I used can be found in the chapter notes at the end of the book.

A great many people helped make this book possible. Many of them, press-shy by professional inclination, discussed stepparenthood with me because they felt that it raised interesting questions that have hardly been examined. Without implying in any way that they share my opinions or my mistakes, I would like to thank the following:

In the United States: Dr. Jesse Bernard, consultant on remarriage, Washington, D.C.; Professor Charles Beye, Classics Department, Boston University; Dr. Lucile Duberman, Sociology Department, Rutgers University; Leon Eisenberg, M.D., chief of psychiatry, Massachusetts General Hospital; Aaron Esman, M.D., New York City; Ursula Gallagher, specialist on adoptions, Children's Bureau, U.S. Department of Health, Education, and Welfare; Paul Glick, senior demographer, U.S. Census Bureau; Dr. William Goode, Sociology Department, Columbia University; Professor Sanford Katz, Boston College Law School; Dr. Nathan Keyfitz, Harvard Center for Population Studies; Norman Robbins, former chairman, Michigan Family Law Committee; Henry Rosner, M.D., Well Baby Center, New York City; Professor Frank Sandler, Harvard Law School; Mrs. Gerda Schulman, Jewish Family Service of New York City; Norman Sherry, M.D., Cambridge, Massachusetts; Arthur Valenstein, M.D., Cambridge, Massachusetts; Professor Walter Wadlington, University of Virginia Law School; and Norman Zinberg, M.D., Cambridge, Massachusetts.

In Britain: The Association of British Adoption Agencies; Louis Blom-Cooper, Q.C., London; Ann Bowden, M.D., London; John Bowlby, M.D., Tavistock Institute for Human Relations; Mrs. Margaret Bramhall, National Council for One-Parent Families; Cabinet de René Chambrun, French lawyers; Church of England Information Office; Mrs. Margaret Cruikshank, *The Economist*; Dr. Ronald Davie, National Children's Bureau; Dr. Esther Goody, New Hall, Cambridge; Dorothy Heard, M.D., Tavistock Institute; Lionel Hersov, M.D., Institute of Psychiatry, Maudsley Hospital; Raymond Hughes, M.D., London; Michael Humphrey, consultant, Atkinson-Morley Hospital; Rabbi Louis Jacobs, New London Synagogue; Peter Laslett, Cambridge Group for the History of Population; Dr. Edmund Leach, provost, King's College, Cambridge; Mrs. Jennifer Levin, senior lecturer on law, Queen Mary College; Drs. Rhona and Robert Rapaport, Institute of Family and Environmental Research; M. L. Rutter, M.D., Institute of Psychiatry, Maudsley Hospital; Anthony Storr, M.D., London; Miss Jean Thompson, Office of Population Censuses and Surveys; and Douglas Woodhouse, Tavistock Institute.

Introduction

This is a decade of stepparents. Every year in the United States, which leads the world in divorce and remarriage, nearly one million children under the age of eighteen see a parent remarry, and well over half a million adults suddenly find themselves to be that curious figure, a stepparent.*

Marrying more than once has never been so popular in contemporary history: one in every three American marriages and one out of every four British marriages is a remarriage for one or both partners. Curiously, marrying a second (or third or fourth) time is a social habit that seems to be gaining ground faster than marriage itself. The rate of first marriage has been declining as more and more young women, because of Women's Liberation, contraception, or disapproval of their mothers' unstable marriages, postpone marriage well into their twenties. But the remarriage rate of widowed and divorced women has risen by 40 per cent during the 1960's and 1970's. During the same years the annual number of divorces has risen by 80 per cent.

The message of the numbers is clear. Never before have people expected so much of marriage. Once they do decide to marry, if they are not happy they dissolve the marriage and enter into another.

And they take their children with them. The women who are now divorcing at record rates are those who married young in the *kinder, küche* 1950's when nobody had heard of Betty Friedan or

* For these calculations, I am indebted to Paul C. Glick, senior demographer, Population Division, Bureau of the Census, and to his colleague, Arthur J. Norton. Some were contributed in private correspondence; others were taken from their paper 'Perspectives on the Recent Upturn in Divorce and Remarriage' (*Demography*, August, 1973), and from Hugh Carter and Paul C. Glick, *Marriage and Divorce: A Social and Economic Study* (Harvard, 1970).

zero population growth. Their penchant for having three, four, or even five babies produced some of the highest fertility rates in American history and is the main reason why there are now record numbers of stepchildren.

At one time children seemed to be a deterrent to divorce. Before 1957 in the United States most divorces occurred among childless couples. Not any more. In the United States, in England, in Australia, in West Germany, France, and Austria, in Scandinavia and Japan – well over half of all divorces are among couples who have children. The number of children involved in the average divorce is rising, too, rising faster than the annual number of divorces. In the United States the average number of children per divorce decree has risen from less than one in the fifties to 1·3 in the seventies.

The precise numbers of stepchildren (or stepparents) are hard to calculate because nobody counts them. "We couldn't if we tried," say people at the U.S. Census Bureau. It is a sensitive subject. Many householders do not want to report that their wife has a child by another husband, or lover, and simply report stepchildren as their own children. Asking embarrassing questions puts the accuracy of all the other answers on the census form in jeopardy and the Census Bureau tries to avoid it.

An educated guess is possible, however. Close to one million American children are involved in divorces every year. If three-quarters of their mothers remarried (as they usually do, within three years), that would make nearly 750,000 stepchildren a year created by divorce alone. But divorce is not the only cause of children acquiring a stepparent.

"Oh, children don't lose fathers and mothers through death any more," an eminent sociologist said glibly. This is a common assumption and it is wrong. While there is no doubt that the percentage of children in the population who have had a parent die has dropped dramatically since the 1920's, the children do exist in great numbers. In the United States each year upwards of 400,000 children lose a parent through death. There even were, at the time of the 1970 census, 50,000 children under the age of ten who were living with a widowed father. The pressure on bereaved parents to remarry – on men especially – needs no description. If even half of them succumb to this pressure, their new marriages would produce about 200,000 stepchildren a year. The supply of stepchildren is also added to by the first marriage of unwed mothers. There are about 400,000 illegitimate births a year, and some of these mothers keep their babies and marry a man who is not the father of the child. Therefore, it is safe to estimate that the yearly American crop of new stepchildren is somewhere around one million.

There is another way to attempt the calculation. The 1970 census showed that there were 12·4 million children under eighteen living with remarried parents. If 65 per cent of these children had been born during the mother's first marriage, as census reports suggest they are, then the national total of stepchildren was then about 8 million. Since the child population in 1970 was 66 million, roughly one in every eight children was a stepchild.

One interpretation of these figures is that in the pursuit of self-fulfillment that marriage is supposed to bring, unprecedented numbers of people find themselves living with other people's children.

CHAPTER I

Something like a witch

It was a chilly English summer night when I first saw my step-children. I parked the car around the corner, as I had been told to do, to escape the eyes of the doctor who lived at the end of the road. Along the short path to the house, the dampness came out to meet me, as if I were going down into a cellar. It was a story-book house, tall and narrow, with a pinched face. Spider webs framed the door. England still was unreal to me, although I had lived in London for nearly a year, and I saw the scene before me as something out of *Great Expectations*. To be honest, my expectations were more than great; they were grandiose. Inside the house were two children, a boy of eight and a girl of five, whose lives I was going to put right.

Their mother had committed suicide about six weeks before. For a dozen years or so, she had lived with the man I was now about to marry. She was not legally his wife; she was somebody else's wife, but where he was, nobody knew. This paper husband had used his power, many years before, to refuse a divorce (as was possible in England until the Divorce Reform Act of 1969), then disappeared and stayed disappeared long after any divorce was wanted.

There was no mistaking it: the house smelled of death. Green lichens grew over the front of the house. Inside, mildew was coming through the walls. The children's mother, who was many years older than their father, had gone through a long decline. From alcohol, sleeping pills, and despair, she had become like a child herself, a bad-tempered child. Two years before her death, the children's father and I had met. We had wanted to get married, but saw it was impossible because of the children and parted. You cannot get a divorce from somebody you're not married to, and if you were an unmarried father at that time, you certainly could not get custody of your children. It was only that summer that we had met again. Although she did not know of our reunion, she realized that the fragile status quo had finally crumbled. One morning she took all her sleeping pills very quickly. The story was reported in detail in the local paper.

I mention these facts at the beginning of my inquiry into step-parenthood, not to confess or to hurt my stepchildren, but rather because I have learned that stepfamilies are, above all, families with a past. Somebody is not there any more. Somebody does not love somebody any more. Stepfamilies live in a different context from the kind of family we consider ordinary, and the basic facts of how and why the husband and wife came to marry (thus making the children stepchildren) matter much more than it matters how Mommy met Daddy.

As I remember it, we asked a psychoanalyst who knew the situation when I should be introduced to the children. His answer was, "When they show signs that they are ready for a new mother." But when was that? You could have said that it was two or three years earlier in their lives. They had been bereft of mothering long before their mother died. For a time while their father was in America, their mother had sent them up to the top floor of the house to live. Do you think I am making this up? It's true. They fed each other, and their mother occasionally, and a boy from the housing estate nearby who often came to play, with baked beans cooked on a toy electric stove. They played outside as late as they wanted, wore what they chose and looked after each other in a robust, fairy-tale way. In one sense, they would never be ready for a new mother, for they had achieved a precocious independence from adults that was to be in their later lives both their greatest strength and their greatest weakness. It was my greatest obstacle as their stepmother.

For a while, we tried to follow the psychoanalyst's advice, and waited for the delicate psychological moment to reveal itself. But then my future husband got the flu, and I put aside the theorizing, not for the last time, and went down to his suburb to visit him. "Do you want to see the children?" he asked. I dreaded it but followed him upstairs. He switched on the overhead light as if he wanted to show me some books or pictures. "Put it out!" I whispered. "You'll wake them up!" He laughed. "Nothing wakes them up," he said. God, he was a confident parent. He was right. They slept on exhibition in bunk beds, healthy, chestnut-haired, freckled-faced survivors of a disaster.

The room had not come through so well. It was a wreck. I tried not to look and saw it all. The light bulb was bare. The blue linoleum was dirty and cracked. The bedclothes were a jumble of rough blankets and gray sheets, and there was the sour smell of bed-wetting. Clothes were everywhere. A sock hung out of a sweater sleeve, an apple core was in a shoe. There was a flimsy cupboard, but what garments it did hold were thrown in a heap at the bottom. In the hall there was an enormous mirror, big enough for a ballet school; one corner was broken off. In the next room a pretentious console table, with flaking gilt cherubs for thighs, surveyed more squalor. Under it was a large wicker basket full of clothes. Hers.

"You couldn't have had a harder job," commented a child psychiatrist whom I interviewed for this book. (Some were far better at getting my story than I was at getting theirs.) On the contrary, I said. As a stepmother, I had ideal conditions. The deluge was over and there I was. Everybody was waiting for someone to come in and play mother and get an orderly life going at last. There was nothing I could do but improve upon the past, and what is more, since I was still unmarried at the advanced age of twenty-eight, I saw the situation as one in which a marriage would make four people happy instead of two. I was eager.

If you were going to meet your new mother this afternoon, what would you want her to wear? I put the question to myself as I nervously prepared to meet the children in the daytime. Finally I decided on a white shirtwaist dress with small red dots. That, combined with red shoes and a green Volkswagen, would, I thought, suggest someone agreeably young, friendly, capable, and pretty (but not too sexy). I knew I was supposed to be good with children, or so my friends had told me as I played with theirs over drinks while they consoled me on my spinsterly state. Girls nowadays cannot know what it was like to be over twenty-one and unmarried in the 1950's. Moreover, I had taken two psychology courses at Radcliffe and had learned a tremendous amount about the dangers of early toilet training and the puritanism of parents who cannot recognize an Oedipus complex when they see it.

My education had not prepared me for my stepdaughter. A plump, poised five-year-old, with a ponytail and a blue pinafore, her first words to me were uttered as she wriggled into her father's lap. "I don't know what you call them," she said, aiming the words right at me, "but I know they're there." Was it an anatomical reference? It was. "She's very precocious," her father explained. Then she ate three of the four peaches (a luxury in England) I had brought as a gift. The boy, thinner and handsome in a hollow-eyed sort of way, stared right through me when we were introduced. He said nothing, as he was engaged in a favorite sport of his, which was running through the house, in the front door and out the back, with a friend named Kevin. I looked for external signs of trauma. There were none. The kids were just busy. In a while, the little girl left her father's lap and went out into the garden. She turned over some kitchen chairs, and by putting a blanket over them, made a house. No sooner was it finished than her brother knocked it flat. "Stop him!" she screamed. "He's spoiling my house!" "Stop him!" I echoed. "She's right! She just got it done when he ruined it!"

In five minutes we had sketched out the lines of our relationship as we would live it for the next ten years. Right away, I failed to be neutral. I took sides. Not always the same side, to be sure, but I could never settle a fight without assigning guilt. She could outtalk me. He gave me visions of Attila the Hun. I kept running to my husband to bail me out. We became like three children with one parent, instead of two children and two parents, and of the children, I often felt the youngest.

That day I slumped home and tried not to think of life after the wedding. "I don't think they liked me very much," I said on the telephone later. "Oh, yes, they did," was the answer. "I heard him threatening his sister that if she didn't lend him sixpence, he would tell you not to let her ride in your Volkswagen."

We had a happy wedding. The children fell ravenously on each present as it arrived. They had new clothes. My stepdaughter had a white, yellow, and blue dress with lace, which she referred to as "my wedding dress," and "wedding shoes" of shiny black. My stepson had his hair cut and, in a gray flannel suit with short trousers, dashed around so assiduously at the reception serving champagne that my old editor from Fleet Street asked, "Who *is* that marvelous little boy?" My new suburban neighbors came, as well as all our friends. My husband's parents beamed throughout and took the children home at the end, so that we could go to France for a week.

We decided to keep the house and not to sell it to the doctor who wanted it, because the school was across the street and because we didn't have the money to move. We had the house painted, the inside at least. The green mold had to stay on the face of the house until spring; there was no point scraping it off at the beginning of an English winter. The children chose new wallpaper for their rooms, and an unwed mother, who did some of the wallpapering, took away the basket of clothes. She was delighted, she said, to have them. With the same brisk air, a prim lady answered our advertisement for a daily cleaning woman. She maintained that she preferred to work on a house that was really dirty. At the end of November we had our first Thanksgiving dinner, and at Christmas a very big tree. My youngest aunt, who was spending a sabbatical year in Paris, came over for Christmas, laden with presents for the children, big ones for under the tree and small presents for the stockings. The children greeted her as if she had always been their aunt.

But it was hell much of the time. The cat left home almost as soon as I arrived. She moved in with our most meddlesome neighbor. The children fought with each other virtually all the time that they were not throwing individual tantrums. They ate candy nonstop, although their teeth were rotted to the bone, and the only way to stop them was to cut their meager allowance so that they could not buy it at the shop around the corner. They resisted the idea of mealtimes, and when they did sit down they often protested about the food. "What's that?" asked my stepson, recoiling when I brought to the table a Yorkshire pudding that had fallen flat. "It's Yorkshire pudding 'orrible," answered his sister.

One particularly bad day there was the Orange Fight. I had closeted myself in our room, trying to finish an article (I had given up my reporting job to work at home because I knew working mothers were bad for children), and left them downstairs with some friends and a bowl of oranges. First they ate the oranges, then they threw the pulpy skins at the newly painted walls. I think I had hysterics.

The worst time of all was during the school vacation that began before Christmas and ran halfway through January. The weather was gray and wet and the children would start fighting before breakfast as the empty day loomed ahead. One morning when my husband tried to escape to his office, I ran out of the house weeping: "You can't leave me here with those children!"

I felt so guilty. Wasn't motherhood what I said I wanted during all those years of waiting? True, I did not think of myself as the children's real mother, but I did think of myself as "a mother." It took one of my stepdaughter's small friends to tell me what I really was. I was driving the two girls home from a birthday party and was deep in my fantasy of myself as a suburban matron, chauffeuring a carload of kids, while they were silent in the back. Suddenly the friend asked, in a crystal English voice, "Is that your *stepmother*?" The answer came, slightly shaky: "Yes." There was a pause. "Oh. I always thought a stepmother was something like a witch."

Witch indeed. What miscasting. I was Snow White, sweeping away the cobwebs and making gooseberry pies.

It took about four months before I saw that I had indeed turned into a witch. Bad-tempered ("Don't they ever go to bed?" I snapped at my husband), guilt-spreading, mean, petty, greedy, self-pitying. Every fault I had seemed to be teased out and magnified by my stepchildren. (Why had the cat left home?) Through it all my husband was patient and uncritical. There were times in that first year when he was the only one left at the table, everybody else having fled in a rage or in tears. He felt somebody had to hold the family together, and besides, he enjoys his dinner.

Stepparenthood brings out the difference between marriage and parenthood. My husband and I could not have been better suited, although we had grown up thousands of miles apart. We were good at school, loners, readers, escapers from poor ambitious families and from claustrophobic small towns that had given us an incurable preference for city life. After time spent in academia, his much longer than mine, we had discovered the guilty delights of journalism. We might have been matched by computer.

But the children and I were a mismatch. My father had died when I was very young; I thought that would make a bond between me and my stepchildren. How wrong I was. Brought up in Massachusetts with my mother's Italian family, and with Irish relatives who sent prayers through the mail, I was weepy and sentimental about death. Memorial Day was the great festive day of the year in my home town; my friends and I trooped merrily over the graves with bunches of wilted lilacs. But my stepchildren were not interested in death, or in their past. In Yeats's phrase, they cast a cold eye; in Nixon's, they toughed it out. There were two of them – that was the big difference – and they had an alliance that made the demands of the rest of the world seem unimportant.

What is more, they had been brought up anarchically. Their mother at her best was spiritedly unconventional and followed a Rousseauean philosophy of child-rearing that holds all rules to be bad. My stepchildren, even without the trauma of their lives, would have seen a laundry basket as a symbol of repression. I, on the other hand, though I had discarded religion, believed in rules and deferred pleasures, in all A's, in brushing your teeth up and down and not sideways, in not eating before mealtime and not opening presents (no, not even one) before Christmas morning. I believed in a "nice home"; they believed a house was a machine for living in, and their machine at that.

Why did we get along at all, you might ask? Because they introduced me to the real world of childhood and because they made me laugh. Also, for their part, because they appreciated my competence and the order I brought. They were glad to have a mother figure they could take out in public. They would lash out at me for hours and then demand that I go to both school plays –

hers in the morning, his in the afternoon – and get there early, to be sure to get a seat in the front row. They taught me the strong verbs of English as it is spoken in England: "He spat at me!" "Well, she trod on my foot!" And they taught me Cockney: "It's the 'olidays, so I uses me bad accent, mate," said my stepdaughter, explaining the sudden change in her diction one day. With tremendous vitality, they collected everything from stamps to horse-chestnuts to numbers printed on the sides of London buses. They made a magnificent dummy for Guy Fawkes Day and gleefully tossed it on the bonfire on the fifth of November. "Good-bye, Guy!" they shrieked, hopping up and down. ("I feel a little sorry for Guy," said my aunt, who was visiting and who, like me, had grown fond of the straw man.) They had a great capacity for enjoying things that were less than perfect – a picnic in the rain, an English beach, a surprise that turned out to be a new pair of socks. I really admired them, but how I wished they lived somewhere else.

A year passed and still I had not "won them over," as the women's magazines had led me to believe I would in time. It was obvious to me that there could be no thought of having a baby myself until I could learn to get along with the two children under the roof. The second year went by and harmony was no closer. I could see that I was too inflexible to be a mother, and by this time I did accurately think of myself as their mother, for I had adopted them in court. They were mine, just as if I had gotten them pink from an orphanage.

Suddenly (Why? My mother had died; I had turned thirty. Who knows?), having a baby became the only thing I wanted to do. And what a revelation pregnancy was. It meant changing in every cell over long, slow months. Even before the baby was born, I could not remember myself as somebody who had never been pregnant. Then I found that motherhood was easy (if you can write off the first few weeks). Everything was on my side – my own memories, instinct, the advice of friends and, of course, Spock. When I tried solutions, they worked. Just as I hated myself as a stepmother, I loved the picture of myself as a mother that floated back at me. When the headmaster of my step-

MOUNT MARY COLLEGE LIBRARY
Milwaukee, Wisconsin 53222

children's school crossed the road one day to say, "You have done wonders with those children," I avoided his eyes. "If he only knew," I thought. The fights, the tears, the sheer blind hate, the sneak eating of a last piece of cake so that *they* would not get it. But when a pediatrician said of my own baby when she was fourteen weeks old and thrusting to stand up, "You have done a good job," I warmed to the compliment. I knew he was right.

My stepchildren are grown up now, good-looking, educated, pleased with themselves. Sometimes I think that bringing them up may turn out to have been my life's major achievement. But I was not a good stepmother. I do not mean that I was a wicked stepmother, nor that they would have turned out better if they had been under someone else's care. I simply mean that we, the three of us, never got it right during more than a decade of family life together. The arguments never went away; only the subjects changed. I was too inexperienced and inflexible to enjoy the job I was doing. They never fell into the rhythm of the home I was trying to establish. They fought it all the way even while they were benefiting from it. And it is only after more than a decade, in which the family constellation has altered completely, that our relationship approaches something that in a guarded way might be called love.

Why? The circumstances, you might say, explain everything and there is no need to look further. My stepchildren had had a troubled early life. I was immature and from a different culture. But I think that there was more to the problem than the particular quirks the children and I happened to have. We did not know what we were aiming at. Neither did my husband. It appears, moreover, that no one else, not other stepparents, not psychologists, anthropologists, or family lawyers, is very clear either.

76-1183

CHAPTER 2

More than kin

KING: But now my cousin Hamlet, and my son –
HAMLET [aside]: A little more than kin and less than
kind!

Hamlet, Act I, Scene ii

A stepparent enters the most ambiguous relationship in what sociologists call the nuclear family. In one sense, the stepparent is a stranger. There is no blood tie between stepparent and step-child, and there is not even that sense of family that binds together uncles, aunts, and cousins whether they like one another or not. The stepparent does not acquire a parent's legal rights over a stepchild. Yet, on the other hand, the stepmother or stepfather has become the person closest to the closest relative a child can have. He or she is in the center of the inner family circle, with all that implies in physical and emotional proximity to a child.

The fact that stepparenthood begins on the wedding day would in itself be sufficient to justify the relationship's troubled reputation. A new marriage is difficult enough without the complication of an instant family. Moreover, most people who become step-parents, whether full-time or part-time, are not thinking very hard about the children when they get married. The children are – and many stepparents used the same phrase to me – "part of the package deal." They are incidental to the marriage, but often not for long. For stepparents have acquired a status ridden with powerful myths and contradictory expectations and with no clear obligations at all.

No wonder that stepparents spend a great deal of time trying to define their relationship to their stepchildren, with results that are seldom satisfying. Even the law is vague about what a step-parent actually is. The *step-* terms are never used in either civil or ecclesiastical law. Instead, the law refers to the "mother's husband" or the "father's wife." Legally speaking, a stepparent is a nonparent. But the law has ways of treating the relationship, whatever it may be, as more permanent than the marriage that created it.

Hamlet's description of a stepparent can hardly be improved upon. A classic stepson, given to muttering to himself, Hamlet brushed off his stepfather-uncle's attempt to call him "son." His stepfather was "more than kin" but "less than kind." In a pun, Shakespeare conveys the contradiction inherent in stepparenthood. The king is closer than a mere relative, but he is not Hamlet's own flesh and blood; neither is he kind. The myth of the cruel stepparent is thus invoked, even before Hamlet learns from the Ghost that the stepfather has murdered his father. (To think of a stepparent as a murderer is a favorite fantasy of stepchildren.)

Modern stepparents fumble and hesitate when they try to find the right word for their role. Some see themselves as approximations of other kinds of relative: "I try to act like a much older brother"; or, "We are close, but not too close – something like cousins." Some search for the telling phrase: it is "an accidental relationship"; or, "it is a phony nonrelationship." Others heartily throw themselves into the role of new mother or new father. Sometimes the children want this, and sometimes, like Hamlet, they emphatically do not. "One thing he won't take from me," said a young stepmother of her husband's adolescent son, "is if I come on like a mother."

One way out of the uncertainty is to deny that any formal relationship exists. Many people who marry someone with children from a previous marriage believe that a stepparent can only be the kind that exists in fairy tales, a replacement for a parent who has died. They argue that as long as there is a natural parent of the same sex alive and able to be father or mother to the child, the new spouse of the other parent is not a stepparent.

This argument does not fit the facts. I have found that the world has such powerful expectations of parenthood and places so many responsibilities on parents that some of these rub off almost inevitably onto any stepparent. Regardless of the circumstances of the marriage, the spouse of a parent will often be required to act like a parent. The demand may come from the spouse, from the stepchild, from a school or a summer camp or doctors, from grandparents, or from welfare agencies. Often, in subtle ways, stepparents demand quasi-parenthood of themselves. Take the following example. A young scientist who had just ended a flamboyant spinsterhood by marrying a divorced man with three daughters told me:

> I'm not a *real* stepmother. Francis's girls live with his ex-wife. They only come to us for vacations. Look, there's one of my step-daughters over there! The little girl passing the wine. . . . I've no problems with them at all, none at all. Thanks to their mother. She's terrific. But of course if their mother should fall under a bus and they came to live with us all the time . . . if I had to tell them to do this and not do that, things might be different.

She gave the lie to her own reasoning. She did not want to consider herself in the role of mother to her husband's children. But she accepted and enjoyed filial behavior from the children: "We couldn't have given the party without her." More than that, she acknowledged that, as New Wife, she is the understudy, the spare mother if anything should happen to the original.

There is reason to believe that children consider any spouse of their parent to be at least their part-parent. They also consider any home where one of their parents is living as one of their homes. Many stepparents who thought they were marrying some-one totally free of past marriages have had a surprise, if the child is old enough to travel alone. Two stepmothers, neither of whom had been married before, told me virtually identical tales:

> Two days after the wedding, there she was on the doorstep. It was her Easter vacation from college and she felt like coming to Boston. She stayed the whole three weeks, and she's coming back in the summer. Funny, she hadn't come near us the whole two years we were living together.

My stepson, who's fourteen, wrote and said he wanted to try living in England for a while. He's been with us five months now. I don't really mind, but we haven't had much chance to be by ourselves since we got married. He says he doesn't like England but he says he's not ready to go back to America yet.

Defining the terms

The definition of stepparenthood accepted by most major dictionaries is a broad one and encompasses remarriages that follow a divorce as well as those that follow widowhood. It is essentially this: "A stepparent is the spouse of one's natural parent by a subsequent marriage." A stepparent, in other words, is someone who has married a parent. No more, no less. It has nothing to do with where the child lives or how old he is or how his own parents' marriage was terminated. It has to do only with remarriage.

The word "subsequent" is important. If you are a woman whose first husband marries again, his new wife (the spouse of the subsequent marriage) becomes stepmother to your children; but you do not become a stepmother to hers by him. Take an example. Nelson Rockefeller is stepfather to the children of his wife's first marriage to Dr. Edward Murphy. His wife, Margaretta Fitler Murphy Rockefeller, is stepmother to the grown Rockefeller children from his first marriage. But his ex-wife, Mary Todd Rockefeller, is not stepmother to the two youngest Rockefeller boys. The French language makes the same distinction. A stepmother is *seconde femme du père*, the second wife of the father. Stepchildren are *enfants d'un lit antérieur*, children of a previous bed. The children by someone else must exist before the marriage if they are to be considered stepchildren. There is another word for children who are begotten outside an existing marriage: bastards.

These must be considered only as working definitions. The lack of consensus about the step-relation is astonishing. Sociologists disagree, dictionaries often contradict themselves. *The Random House Dictionary of the English Language*, for example, defines a stepmother as "one who takes one's mother's place by marriage to one's father." This implies that a stepmother is active as a substitute mother. But the same dictionary describes a step-child as "a child of one's husband or wife by a former marriage." There is no suggestion of bereavement, and the definition would apply equally to stepchildren who never set eyes on the stepparent. French usage seems to be even more confused. Several diction-aries, while clearly defining stepparents as the spouse of a parent, go on to describe a stepbrother as *un frère consanguin ou demi-frère* – a half brother or blood brother. That is just what step-brothers are not. If you have a half brother, you share a parent and therefore have a blood tie. But a stepbrother is merely the son of your stepparent.

The confusion between stepchildren and bastards is apparent in Greek mythology. The goddess Hera, the wife of Zeus, was full of wrath against the many children sired by her promiscuous husband. Her malice is often described as stepmotherly. But as she was already the wife of Zeus when most of the infidelities took place, Hera cannot be considered a true stepmother, although in spirit she is the prototype of wicked stepmothers in Western civilization. One scholar, trying to get around the problem while summarizing the plot of Euripides' *Madness of Hercules*, called Hercules, who was the son of Zeus by Alcmene, the "bastard stepson" of Hera:

> Hera, the Queen of Heaven, ever jealous of her bastard stepson, sends Madness with her snake's hair against him, so that in frenzy he murders his wife and sons.

It was a wicked trick for Hera to play; none the less, "bastard stepson" is a contradiction in terms.

I will not apologize further for using the definition "spouse of one's parent by a subsequent marriage," for I have found that it is the definition in general usage and that most people who have acquired stepchildren through divorce think of themselves as stepparents. The sheer fact that one has to choose a meaning among alternatives shows how unsure current society is about stepparenthood. There is no confusion about what "mother" and "father" mean.

Are they relatives?

There are two ways in which human beings can be related in the legal sense – by blood or by marriage. Blood relatives are called consanguineous, relatives by marriage affinal. Stepparent and stepchild are not mere acquaintances, as some choose to think. They are affinal relatives because of the stepparent's marriage with the children's biological parent. In fact, the remarriage of anybody with children creates a special set of affinal relations for the new spouse and the children involved. There are step-brothers, stepsisters, stepgrandparents, and stepaunts, and step-uncles. True, these labels are rarely used, but they have meaning and we can figure out what the relationship is. What stepparent-hood is, in actuality, is a form of kinship, a fact illustrated by the prohibition of marriage between stepparent and stepchild. That prohibition is a relic of the past, yet it is a kinship taboo just as much as those observed by primitive tribes and it has subtle effects on contemporary stepparents.

To try to understand the exact form of the tie between step-parent and stepchild is no idle exercise. Stepchildren themselves want to know. My own stepson, two days after arriving in Massachusetts to meet my family, spent hours drawing family trees in which he tried to integrate his family with mine. A similar story was told me by a young stepmother, whose husband had been married twice before. His eleven-year-old daughter by his first wife loved to visit her father in his new home; she liked her stepmother and enjoyed playing with the new babies. One day the girl drew a picture of a house in which all her father's wives and all his children were under the same roof, looking out of different windows. On another visit she drew her father and her step-mother standing together, and then extended out from them on either side all the children they had produced. (This marriage itself was breaking up, and the husband's first wife had tele-phoned the stepmother to say that she hoped there would be no divorce because "yours is the only stable home my daughter has ever known.")

It is often said that divorce and remarriage are so common these days that children are quite accustomed to having several fathers and several mothers. Having them, perhaps. But it is not clear to me that they are equally resigned to losing them. Children may, much more than adults realize, consider themselves somehow related to all the people their parents choose to marry.

What stepparenthood is not

Time and time again, people confuse stepparenthood with adoption. A typical comment was offered to me enthusiastically by a radio broadcaster sophisticated enough to know better:

> Stepparents – what a fascinating subject! My sister is a stepmother. She and her husband couldn't have any children of their own and then they got this Korean war orphan. That was fifteen years ago and now are they having their problems!

or, from a scientist:

> Being a stepparent must be just like adopting. Oh, all right, the motives may be different at the beginning. But after that, the feelings involved are the same as in adoption.

Adoption and stepparenthood, as a matter of fact, differ in almost every significant detail. The fact that many stepparents go to court and adopt their stepchildren (as I did) simply underlines the fact that they are two separate kinds of relationship and that adoption achieves certain legal objectives that stepparenthood does not begin to touch. Some of the emotional differences are glaring to anybody who has talked with both kinds of parent. Stepparents, by and large, think of their role as a duty. They may like it, they may hate it or feel inadequate, but they carry a sense of obligation about it and often refer to it as "a job". While the stepparent usually just wants to get married, adoptive parents (at least those who adopt strange children rather than the children of relatives) have put in long emotional preparation for a child. As one man who had adopted two children, as well as made a career as an expert in adoption, expressed it: "I have never thought of adopting a child as a job. To me, it is self-fulfillment." Not many stepparents would say that.

The difference between the two roles is so stark that I can illustrate it in two lists.

Adoption

1. Adoption involves a change in legal status.
2. It is permanent.
3. The adopting couple have a marriage of proven stability.
4. They both want a child.
5. They stand at the same distance from the child (unless they are adopting a child who is a relative).
6. They acquire an infant or young child with little memory of its parents.
7. They receive professional guidance on possible emotional problems ahead.
8. Their act is seen by society as kind and generous.

Stepparenthood

1. The stepparent has no legal rights over the stepchild.
2. The relationship usually dissolves with the marriage creating it.
3. Stepparenthood is simultaneous with the new marriage.
4. The fertility of the new marriage is usually untested.
5. The stepparent stands in opposite relation to the child and spouse, as one is the biological parent and the other a stranger.
6. The stepchild usually knows or remembers the parent whom the stepparent replaces.
7. There is virtually no professional guidance offered to the stepparent.
8. The stepparent is burdened with an ancient and unflattering myth.

While clearing up common confusions, I might as well deal with foster parents. To foster means literally to nourish and to feed, and more generally, to support and to bring up with parental care. Particularly in the past, a man's new wife could often be properly described as a foster mother, for she brought up a stepchild as her own. The term now is usually used to describe formal arrangements, normally backed by law, in which a couple, or a woman, looks after a child who needs a home in exchange for payment. Foster homes are intended to be temporary (although many foster parents come to love their foster children and want to adopt them – the root of many headline-making court fights between the foster parents and the natural parent). Suffice it to say that "foster mother" has a pleasing ring while "stepmother" does not.

If families in which there is a stepparent differ from adoptive families, they differ far more from ordinary families. The reason is that the basic rules that govern family life are disturbed in families where the children are not the biological offspring of both the husband and wife in the household. These rules concern sex and money: who may have sexual relations with whom, who must support whom and who may inherit from whom. Father sleeps with a woman who is not his son's mother and is therefore not explicitly forbidden to the son by the recognized incest taboo. The child sits at the table of the breadwinner of the household, but the child is actually supported by a father living somewhere else. Often children who ordinarily would expect to inherit from their father and mother find their parent's new spouse will take away some or all of what might have been their portion. Or, if there are children of the new marriage as well as of a former marriage, there often exists an uncomfortable situation in which there are two sets of children who live under the same roof, or who spend vacations together, but who have quite different financial expectations. One might be, say, the daughter of the late Aly Khan and the other of Orson Welles.

This asymmetry can be accentuated by the grandparents. Half-siblings have one set of grandparents in common and another set that is not mutual. This leads to the kind of scenario described by a stepmother whose young stepdaughter had, alone of anybody in the family, the prospect of wealth:

> We haven't told any of them yet that Elizabeth is going to get her grandparents' money, but our children have been visiting there and seen the paintings and we think that all three children have realized it somehow.

As accepted as divorce is now, remarriage disturbs the family pattern of sexual and property rights just as much as in the past. Still, there is no model for how a stepparent should behave. The parent's obligations, by contrast, are clear. The anthropologist Bronislaw Malinowski has pointed out that "the mother, besides feeling inclined to do all she does for her child, is none the less obliged to do it." Stepparents often do not feel inclined to do anything for their stepchildren, yet they feel strong pressure from the community, and from their spouse, to do something. But what? For natural parents, not only the obligations but the ideals are clear. The world believes that parenthood is a task that can and should be done well. Dr. Spock's best-known book has sold many millions of copies because people want guidance on achieving the ideals, and because they believe, as a corollary, that if they do it badly, their children will be depressed or delinquent.

The social questions posed by the remarriage of parents have hardly been faced by a society that ostensibly accepts divorce as the right solution to an unhappy marriage. We have been told that the marriage bond is the structural keystone in our kinship system and that our identity depends entirely on the marriage unit (apart from a few recognized family clans, like the Kennedys, Rockefellers, and Rothschilds). Who we are depends entirely on two families – our family of origin and our family of procreation; we are the children of our parents and the parents of our children. But we are not told how to preserve our sense of identity if we have a mother in one family, a father in another, a son in a third, and a daughter in a fourth.

The problems of identity and confused responsibilities are critical for children and adults who live in families that are amalgams of other families, and begin to explain why stepparenthood is nothing like parenthood. The clarity of family life is absent in stepfamilies, and undefined relationships in close quarters do not make for easy living.

Variations of parenthood

After considering what stepparenthood is not, it is now time to see why a stepparent should be treated as a species of parent at all. One reason is social pressure. When it is convenient to treat a stepparent as a parent, all kinds of organizations do, even if the letter of the law disagrees. For example, the U.S. Department of Labor defines as "own" children of the head of the family sons, daughters, stepchildren, and adopted children, but not others, such as nieces, nephews, or grandchildren. Many social agencies follow the same practice. To them, children fall into two categories: those living with two parents and those living with one.

These agencies, in particular, should know better than to put a parent substitute in the same class as a natural parent when they are, for example, describing a home that has produced a battered child or a sexually abused child. But still they persist. Replacements are counted as the real thing. It is the rare stepparent who can opt for the role of nonparent. School concerts and camp visiting days are full of stepparents who do not dare to say, "But I'm not a parent."

Another reason to consider the stepparent a form of parent is that there are many ways of being a parent without physically producing a child. What anthropologists call "fictive parenthood" can be a powerful bond. *The Godfather* was more than the story of the way the Mafia works. It was an illustration of fictive parenthood, of a man going to excessive lengths to keep his vow to advance his godson in life. Almost everybody acts like a parent to somebody – most of us to our own parents if they live long enough. A homosexual once spoke to me movingly about his godchildren. They are as close to parenthood as he will ever get, and whenever someone refers to children or the feelings of parents, he thinks of them. For him, they are his children. Most people who marry a parent will feel something of this pull on their store of parental feelings.

Many of the stepparents whose words appear in this book give evidence of having played parental roles, often unconsciously. The stepmother who buys extra Kleenex because the stepchildren, visiting for the weekend, have runny noses is nursing them in a maternal sense. The stepfather who gives the wife's grown-up children a list of introductions in a new city is sponsoring them into adult status, whether he knows them well or not. (An Italian journalist, who delivered to me a savage condemnation of the stepfather in his life, admitted: "One thing he did for me – he taught me to climb mountains. But," he added, "he only did it for his own pleasure, I think.") Teaching a stepchild something may be one of the best ways for a stepparent to reach a stepchild, for it allows the stepparent to display qualities he or she values as a person without involving an artificial assumption of parental behavior. The stepparent and the natural parent decide between them which activities within the family are linked with biological parenthood and which with sex. When the visiting stepchild cries in the night, who gets up, the father or the woman?

To recapitulate, stepparents and stepchildren are related through the marriage of the stepparent to the children's natural parent. But what follows from that is not clear, legally, financially, or sexually. Stepparents are torn between conflicting ideals: that they be no more than a parent's spouse and that they be in some undefined way an approximation of a parent, that they be both no parent and new parent. Their dilemma is the result of the social contradiction succinctly described by Margaret Mead:

> We have constructed a family system which depends upon fidelity, lifelong monogamy, and the survival of both parents. But we have never made adequate social provision for the security and identity of the children if that marriage is broken, as it so often was in the past by death or desertion, and as it so often is in the present by death or divorce. We have, in fact, as did the primitive Mundugumor, Arapesh and Dobuan, saddled ourselves with a system that won't work.

CHAPTER 3

By any other name

The words "stepparent" and "stepchild" carry such overtones of hatred, deprivation, and murder ("Snow White" and "Hansel and Gretel" are stories of failed murder attempts) that many people refuse to use them. Professionals do not agree on what is the best practice. One child psychiatrist from Manhattan who is often consulted by parents changing partners says, "I never use the words 'stepmother' or 'stepfather.' I simply talk about New Mommy and New Daddy." A social worker from the Jewish Family Service in New York, who believes the *step-* words are more accurate, uses them deliberately, but acknowledges that "they are still powerful nasty words." The sociologist Dr. Jesse Bernard, who wrote what is perhaps the only full-length study of remarriage, rejected *step-* terms, "for they are, in effect, smear words," and substituted "acquired children" and "acquired parents." Such euphemisms are awkward and are unlikely to pass into popular usage. Stepfamilies find themselves pondering terminology over and over again, and inevitably, even if only occasionally, they fall back on stepmother, stepfather, stepson, and stepdaughter, for, like it or not, these are the words for the thing.

The dilemma symbolizes how the stepparent is torn between the roles of nonparent and new parent. The alternatives, in terminology as in so much of the relationship, seem to be between pretending on the one hand and hurting the child's feelings on the other. It is wrong to be false and also wrong to cause pain to a child. There can be little doubt that some stepchildren feel sensitive to reminders of what they see as an irregular status. A psychiatric study of stepchildren by Dr. Edward Podolsky revealed that "children apologize, even tell lies to conceal the fact that they have a stepparent." Because of this, "many children who acquire stepparents in infancy are not told."

The main difficulty in dropping the prefix *step-* and referring to a stepchild as one's own child is that if the truth comes out, as it has a way of doing, then it looks as if the step-relation is really something to be ashamed of, as if the child is in some way déclassé, and as if the stepparent is pretending to a false status.

I fell into this trap early. About a year after my marriage, my mother had a stroke. I had to go home to Massachusetts in a hurry, and my stepdaughter, then aged six, begged to come along. She was afraid I would not come back. Sympathetic, and wanting to show her off, I took her along. She was duly idolized and then, after a couple of days, bitten by the family dog. (Would he have bitten my own child?) I rushed to the local hospital and presented her as my daughter. Why bother with subtle kinship terms at a time like that? "All right," said the head nurse, "when did she last have a tetanus shot?" I didn't know. "Has she ever had one?" I didn't know that either. "Well, what kind of mother are you?" she asked, and people looked up. "A stepmother," I had to confess, and the folly of not being open about stepparenthood swept over me. It was obvious that the child and I did not make a pair; our coloring, even our accents, were different. Since then I have referred to her as my stepdaughter. But she interprets that as rejection. "Why tell everybody?" she says.

There simply is no invariable rule. A young social worker was surprised one day to be scolded by her own sister for calling her stepchildren "stepchildren." The sister had reason to be sensitive to the term for she had remarried and her own son had become a stepchild. "The children don't like it," the sister said, and the social worker, conscientious about children's feelings, decided to take an instant poll of the children around the table. It was true; they did not like to be called stepchildren, although they all were, and so the social worker stopped using the term. Until, that is, the day when she had to call up a camp for Jewish girls to ask for a place for her "daughter." "Are you Jewish?" asked the voice at the other end. "No, I'm not a bit Jewish," she replied, "but my husband is Jewish and his first wife is Jewish and my daughter could not be more Jewish."

Is it worth trying to disguise such basic facts of family life in order to pretend to a child that it has lost nothing important because the parents have divorced and remarried? In such cases stepparents often feel that neither course of action seems right. Here again, the contrast with adoption is marked. A pamphlet given to one of my neighbours in London, an adoptive parent, anticipates the problem and gives firm advice:

> Overemphasizing adoption can make children uncomfortable. It should be up to them to divulge private facts about themselves to their friends, and they definitely do not want to be introduced as "our adopted girl" or "my adopted son." You may be doing this from pride and pleasure, but the child could well feel that you are pointing him out as less than a complete member of the family.

Why can adoption workers speak with such confidence? Because the terms of the relationship are clear. Adopted children are "own" children. Through the legal procedure of adoption, all the legal rights and obligations that formerly existed between the child and his natural parents come to an end and are replaced by similar rights and obligations with respect to his new adoptive parents. The adoptive mother is rightly called "mother" and the adopted girl "daughter." There is no need for stammering.

Origin of the terms

The link with death is old and undeniable. All the *step-* words trace their origin to the Old English *stēop-*, which is linked with words for bereavement. A stepchild was a *stēopbearn*, an orphan; a stepparent, the new spouse of a widowed parent. The original association, therefore, is with the greatest pain a child can experience, the loss of a parent and the loss of the central place in the surviving parent's affections. In an oblique way, the overtones of rejection carried by the *step-* prefixes are accentuated, I think, by the ordinary meaning of the word "step": a step away, one step removed. The word "stepparent" suggests somebody who is a step in distance from the child and a degree less loving, less committed, than a natural parent. The *step-* prefix is doubly pejorative.

An intimation that society understands far more than it admits about the tensions of the step-relationship comes from the close ties between the *step-* words and the *-in-law* words. In English and American usage for about four hundred years, from 1440 until at least the mid-nineteenth century, the term "mother-in-law" was often used to refer to a stepmother. Although such a meaning is now regarded as incorrect, it once made literal sense. A stepmother was a mother "in law," that is, in canon law, by the fact of her marriage to a child's father.

Even today, the psychological resemblances between the two female roles are striking. Both involve an older and a younger woman competing for a man's love. A mother-in-law strives to stay close to her son although he has a bride; a stepmother hopes to keep the attention of a father away from his daughter. The mother-in-law is the only family relation to bear the same opprobrium as the stepmother. Both roles are burdened by myth, although the mother-in-law is a subject for jokes (presumably because her sexual charms are fading) while the stepmother never is. The parallel can be seen in the Grimm brothers' story "The Six Swans," in which first the stepmother, and then the mother-in-law plot against the young princess. In 1540 a religious book for Christian women described the feelings of the one as resembling the other: "It is said, that mothers in lawes beare a stepmothers hate unto their daughters in lawes."

"Mother-in-law," when it was used to mean father's wife rather than spouse's mother, carried all the ugly connotations of the word "stepmother" itself. In Henry Fielding's *Miser*, written in 1732, Mariana says, "I know the word mother-in-law has a terrible sound, but perhaps I may make a better than you imagine." In his diary, the seventeenth-century English clergyman Ralph Josselin wrote that when his mother died when he was only eight, he "feared a mother-in-lawe and undoing by her." His fears were justified, too. His father did remarry, and the new wife was "a woman of sower spirit."

During much of the same period, the term "father-in-law" was also used to mean stepfather. Here again, the term conveyed something of the emotional, as well as the legal, realities of the relationship. For example, George Washington became stepfather and guardian to Jacky and Patsy Custis when he married the rich widow Martha Custis, and in his letters Washington always seems to have referred to his wife's son as "my son-in-law." Washington felt his responsibilities for the boy and his estate to be heavy, for Jacky Custis was more interested in travel and society than in education and insisted on marrying, to Washington's dismay, at the early age of seventeen. Notice how Washington avoids both the terms "son" and "stepson" in this letter offering a clergyman a position as Jacky's tutor:

> Rev. Sir: Mr. Magowan who lived several years in my family, a Tutor to Master Custis (my Son-in-Law and Ward) having taken his departure for England leaves the young Gentleman without any master at this time.

For young women, a stepfather can be a menacing figure who threatens, and sometimes achieves, seduction. Many of the literary references to "father-in-law" carry this sense of menace. In George Eliot's *Daniel Deronda*, a young woman, Gwendolen Grandcourt, in a state of shock after watching her despised husband die in a boating accident, thinks back to her stepfather:

> It came over me that when I was a child I used to fancy sailing away into a world where people were not forced to live with any one they did not like – I did not like my father-in-law to come home.

A possible explanation for calling a stepparent a parent-in-law is to avoid the uglier nuances of the *step-* term. They have been there, particularly for stepmothers, since antiquity. Ovid wrote of the ghastly poisons mixed by vicious stepmothers (*lurida terribiles miscent aconita novercae*). Many other classical writers used the term as a synonym for malevolence and hostility. In Latin *noverca*, stepmother, also came to be used in agriculture, but again it meant nothing good: ditches that drain off water slowly, or rough land.

The French preserve the old practice. A *belle mère*, beautiful mother, can be either a mother-in-law or a stepmother, and it is safe to conclude that *belle* is a blatant euphemism. A stepmother, or a mother-in-law, calls up thoughts that are far from lovely. The cover-up carries through the whole list of step-relations.

The French use *beau fils* for stepson and *belle petite fille* for step-granddaughter, but when they want to convey the idea of stepmother in its full horror – meaning an unnatural or wicked mother – they bring out something much harsher: *marâtre.*

Private names – public faces

A stepfamily has to make certain basic decisions about terminology: (1) What is the stepchild to call the stepparent? A version of Mommy or Daddy, the stepparent's first name, or a special nickname? (2) Are they going to use the *step-* words in introductions, conversations, and other references to their relationship? (3) If children accompany their mother into her new marriage, will they keep their father's last name or switch to the stepfather's name?

For many people, the question of first names is the critical one. "And what do they call you?" people would ask me with that frank curiosity that stepparents arouse. When I replied, "Brenda," their faces would fall. To me, there seemed no alternative; my stepchildren remembered their own mother as Mummy.* Most of the stepparents whom I interviewed took it for granted that their stepchildren would use their first names. But this runs counter to the popular belief that for a child to call a stepparent Mommy or Daddy is a proof that the child has accepted the stepparent. Dr. Spock, who deals with stepparent-hood in one of his lesser-known works, *Problems of Parents,* recognizes this belief and tries to dispel it. He explains that a stepchild, out of loyalty to his own father, may choose not to call his stepfather Father. But, he says, "this should not be felt as a reproach by the stepparent or as a sign of his failure even to a slight degree."

Another expert disagrees. Paul Bohannan, professor of anthropology at Northwestern University, believes that a stepparent's authority in the household may be weakened if the stepchild does not use a parental term of address. He described a girl of nine,

* English and American pronunciations of this word differ and I have used the English spelling when referring to an English voice.

whose mother had married four times, who tried hard to find a special label for each of her "fathers":

> She called her father, the mother's first husband, Daddy. The other three she called Daddy-Tom, Daddy-Dick, and Daddy-Harry. Americans, as is their cultural tradition, usually utilize first names. However, using the first name may undermine a good authority relationship between a stepparent and stepchild and may intensify competitiveness.

The invention of family terminology is an unappreciated art. Almost everybody has to do it. There is no established rule for what to call mothers-in-law, for example, and there is considerable confusion, and jousting for position, as a couple tries to find words for their children to distinguish between the maternal and paternal set of grandparents. (Try asking people what they call their own grandparents and watch them blush. I have collected some rare specimens: Gam-Gam and Gumpy, Pappy and Mémé, Oma and Opa.) One young stepmother, whose stepchildren arrived for a two-month summer visit soon after she married their father, was given a special title: "Miz," a remarkable solution (it was before Ms.) to the children's wish to award her an informal maternal status. And the stepchildren still write to her as "Miz" even though they are grown up.

There are subtle ways of acknowledging two fathers. One girl referred to her dead father as "my father," and to her stepfather, whom she disliked heartily but who paid for her psychoanalysis, as Daddy. The New Testament shows how the distinction can be made by using the same word with different emphasis. When Mary and Joseph realized that the boy Jesus was missing from their band of travelers, they hurried back to Jerusalem and found him in the temple. According to St. Luke:

> His mother said unto him, Son why has thou thus dealt with us? Behold, thy father and I have sought thee sorrowing.

> And he said unto them, How is it that ye sought me? Wist ye not that I must be about my Father's business?

When stepchildren have to live with children of the new

marriage, or when there are stepchildren from both sides of the
new marriage, then the children themselves have to come to an
agreement about which parents get which labels. Many stepmothers report that their own babies call them by their first
name because they hear the stepchildren doing it. Some say they
do not mind; for others, it means that the stepchildren have
unwittingly deprived them of the chance to be called Mommy by
anybody. On the other hand, when you get two sets of children
under the same roof, with one set referring to the woman at the
head of the household as Mommy and the other set calling her
by her first name, you cannot escape the feeling that there is a
hierarchy of children in the household, with those able to use the
Mommy label in the superior position.

When my own children came along, I was sad that my stepchildren had nobody that they could call Mommy. Here is an
ingenious resolution of the problem given me by a widow with
two young daughters who had married a widower with two
slightly older daughters:

> My husband's oldest girl was so relieved to be able to stop looking
> after the house that she began calling me Mommy. But my girls
> called my husband Tom. One day my stepdaughter told them right
> out: "Look, if *she's* Mommy, then *he's* Daddy." It made sense.
> We've been Mommy and Daddy to them all ever since.

Names are so personal that they can provide fertile ground
for hostility between stepparent and stepchild. A stepmother
reminisced, with some amusement, about her mother's second
husband: "We called him 'Cap' because he had been a captain
during the war. For some reason, he absolutely hated it but it
was years before we could call him Dave." (Not long after this,
she stopped speaking to her stepfather at all, because her mother
died and there was a fight about the will.) One stepmother's
difficulties with a tiny stepdaughter are epitomized in the fact that
she and the child have identical first names:

> Well, there's another problem. She has the same name as mine,
> Laura. When her mother died, she went to live with an aunt who
> overfed her and then they all called her Pudgie because she was so

overweight. Obviously we couldn't go on calling her that, and she knew her real name was Laura and we couldn't take that away from her. She'd been through enough upheaval. My husband calls me Mommy to her, but still it's not easy. Having the same name creates the illusion of a link which is not there. And when I hear him calling Laura! I think he means me. I don't like having to share my name.

Private names and affectionate terms define our relationships with our intimates, but our last name tells the world who we are. To be more precise, it declares who our father was. For a woman and her new husband, the different last name of the stepchild is a public admission that she has had another husband. The fact that so many couples, and so many stepchildren, want to peel off the old label and replace it with a new one is a sign that society is not as comfortable about divorce as it pretends.

Dr. Spock, who is so sympathetic to the stepchild who doesn't want to call his stepfather Father, none the less thinks that there is a case for letting the stepchild borrow the stepfather's surname. When a young child acquires a likeable stepfather whose last name is used by everyone else in the family, Dr. Spock says "it is natural that he may want to use it too, to be regular, to belong to the household." He then gives some advice to the absent father:

> If I were the father, I'd let the child use the other name if that made him comfortable. I'd keep his attachment and trust in me by means of regular contacts and other expressions of love.

But natural fathers often are not as equable as Dr. Spock. They may allow a stepfather to raise their child and pay his bills, but become angry when adoption is suggested, which would strip the child of the natural father's name. The desire to change the child's name – to make him "regular" – is one of the prime motives in stepparent adoptions. Although I will discuss this subject more fully in Chapter 11, it is relevant to mention here the reproof given to a stepfather and his wife by a British High Court judge in 1973. The judge found in favor of a natural father who had appealed against a lower court's consent to the adoption of his two girls, aged eight and seven, by their stepfather. The judge failed to see how the adoption would benefit the girls:

> when the expressed object was to give them the mother's new surname. All too often that course was taken by the mother to disguise from her new neighbors that she had been involved in a failed marriage. It could not be by itself a legitimate ground for adoption or generally in the interests of children.

When the stepfamily is comfortable with its past, two last names present no problem. An American stepfather who lives in England described travel with his own children and his stepson:

> It doesn't embarrass us a bit. I give the passport inspector all the passports and I explain the difference in name by saying, "This is Keith Johnson who's traveling with us."

One middle-aged stepfather I interviewed has presided for twenty years over a happy household in which three of his wife's children use the name of their father who was killed in World War II and the younger three, their joint children, use his. Two last names are just a detail of life as this particular family lives it, and the stepfather has never dreamed of asking that the name of the dead father be given up.

As everybody is aware, however, children do not like to be different. They often take their stepfather's name, sometimes surreptitiously. The widow with two daughters who was quoted earlier described it this way:

> When I got married again, the girls were going to keep their father's last name – Merrill – partly to please his parents who had no other children. But when their workbooks came home from school, they had Owen written on them. "Well, if you're going to be Owen, we want to be Owen like you," they said. Then when the passport question came up, it was awkward with them using two different names, so we went to court and changed it.

But one stepfather, with a distinguished family name, complained:

How do other stepparents feel about a strange child taking their name? He just uses my name. He wants it. He won't change his other name legally, and there are all sorts of embarrassments with passports and things. But my family name, well, I suppose I'm ridiculous, but it's an old New England name and I resent him using it.

This man did not object to the fact that the boy, who had lived with him since infancy, called him Daddy.

Steps or children?

Although the world comforts itself with the idea that children may want to call a stepparent Mommy or Daddy, it also distrusts stepparents, partly because it believes the stepparent may be after the stepchild's inheritance. As a result, a stepparent's willingness to call the stepchild son or daughter may be interpreted as a sign of trickery. Shakespeare uses this device as the first sign to the audience that the stepparent is a villain. In *Cymbeline*, the wicked queen, who is scheming to marry her stepdaughter to her own loathsome son so that he will inherit the throne, first addresses her stepdaughter with the very opposite of the truth:

> QUEEN: No, be assur'd you shall not find me, daughter,
> After the slander of most stepmothers,
> Evil-ey'd unto you.

But the stepdaughter, Imogen, will not be fooled:

> IMOGEN: Dissembling courtesy! How fine this tyrant
> Can tickle where she wounds!

Imogen chooses her own way of referring to her father and his new wife: "A father cruel and stepdame false."

The same kind of exchange, with the stepparent concealing and the stepchild asserting the truth, occurs when the king first calls Hamlet son. He begs Hamlet to put aside his grief for his dead father, for it is a sin against nature, "whose common theme is death of fathers." Besides, the king argues, Hamlet has a new father:

KING: We pray you throw to earth
   This unprevailing woe, and think of us
   As of a father, for let the world take note
   You are the most immediate to our throne,
   And with no less nobility of love
   Than that which dearest father bears his son
   Do I impart toward you.

For a stepfather, these sentiments are impeccable. The snag is that the king is lying.

By now it should be clear that dishonesty, like inheritance and sexual rivalry, is a major element in the stepparent stereotype. A stepfather from Manhattan, after years of family life with a boy whose mother he had married when the boy was less than a year old, says carefully: "I make it a point not to call him my son. I say 'my stepson,' even though I am aware it is technical-sounding." What he means is that "stepson" sounds cold and rejecting. But he prefers it to the alternative, which is to pretend to be a father where he is not. George Washington, who reputedly never told a lie, was scrupulous in maintaining the correct verbal distance from his stepchildren. Even when Patsy Custis died in 1773 at the age of seventeen, the Custis children remained Martha's, not George's, as this letter shows:

Mount Vernon, June 20, 1773

Dear Sir: It is an easier matter to conceive, than to describe the distress of this Family; especially that of the unhappy Parent of our Dear Patsy Custis, when I inform you that yesterday removed the Sweet Innocent Girl Entered into a more happy and peaceful abode than any she has met with in the afflicted Path she has hitherto trod. . . .

This sudden and unexpected blow, I scarce need add has almost reduced my poor Wife to the lowest ebb of Misery; which is encreas'd by the absence of her son. . . .

Listen, in contrast, to a young stepmother describing the verbal arrangements in her complicated family structure. Her present husband has several children from his other marriages, and she has one small girl from her first: "Of course, I call my husband's children my stepchildren. What else would I call them? Some of them are older than I am." But does her husband call her own young child his stepdaughter? "Oh, no. She thinks he's her *father*." Such lies are intended to be kindly. Yet they protect the stepparent more than the child (who almost inevitably learns the facts) and are another sign that adults, like children, will go to great lengths to avoid the stigma of the *step-* label. When the lies are practiced socially, without concealing the truth from the child, they may express a wish to show the world that as much love exists as if it were a blood relationship. A middle-aged woman, childless and recently divorced, was quite moved when she went to visit her former husband's son at his university. The young man entered her in the guest book under her old married name and described her as "Mother." Sensing that an explanation was needed, he told her: "I think it helps to have a lot of mothers, don't you?"

All the complicated feelings that stepparents and stepchildren have for each other come out when they introduce each other or describe their relationship. One stepfather, who has three of his wife's children in more or less permanent residence, was intrigued by the question of terminology:

> Now that you mention it, I think I always refer to them as "our children" or "the children," but never as "my" children. If it is something that just involves me and them, like if I was telling a colleague that I was taking them to visit their grandmother, then I call them "my kids."

But then he sat up straight and spoke fiercely:

> Because I do not feel that they *are* my children. They don't look like me. My sister's children look more like me. *They* could be my children.

It is interesting that this man, childless himself, has left the bulk of his inheritance to his sister's children, and expects that his stepchildren will be looked after in their own father's will. Another stepfather in a similar position gets along quite comfortably with the phrase "my wife's children," and occasionally, in conversation, an "our children" slips in. It is possible to use the *step-* terms gracefully. I heard a woman at a dinner party being asked whether her daughter, who was also present, was at college. "Actually, she's not my daughter," was the response. "She's my stepdaughter, but I would be happy to claim ownership."

It would be good if there were a discernible path through this maze of *step-* terminology. Perhaps the *step-* prefixes hurt children less if their parents are divorced and the original mother or father is still available. One woman remembered that her mother "never called my stepsister her stepdaughter. Because my stepsister's real mother was dead. She didn't have any other mother than my mother." But the stepchildren quoted at the beginning of this chapter who minded being called stepchildren all had both natural parents alive and available. And the stepparents I talked with who have raised stepchildren from infancy did not, in general, find that true parental feelings gushed forth, even though they had seen the stepchild's first steps and heard their first words. Many stepparents and some anthropologists call for a new term to refer to "the child of my husband" or "my father's wife's son." But they never suggest any. It is hard to design kinship terms for relationships where the emotional ground is so shaky.

In my family, the conflict was never solved. Often I use the *step-* prefix, sometimes I say son or daughter, and usually I dodge the issue by introducing them flatly by their full names. My stepson evolved his own method of introduction. "This is Ray," he will say to me, and to Ray he says, "This is . . . ," and his voice trails off. To my knowledge, he has never filled in the blank.

This is the heart of the problem. There are no new words, yet for some, the old words like "stepmother" are unspeakable.

CHAPTER 4

Courtship

Courtship, with children in the back of the car, in the next bedroom or the same tent, requires determination. Idealizing each other is part of the pleasure of falling in love, and it is hard to sustain against cries of "I want an ice cream" and a chorus of criticism ("Why do you go out with Shirley? I like Lois better"). It is also hard to preserve when you see the beloved, or the beloved sees you, shouting at a child. Perhaps that is what relatives and friends mean when they tell someone about to marry a parent: "I suppose you know what you're getting into." They assume that much of the romance has been conducted in laundromats, zoos, assembly halls, and bathrooms, places where people who have children spend a lot of their time, and where everyone has been seen at his worst.

All courtship systems are "market or exchange systems," according to Professor William Goode of Columbia University. They differ from one another, he says in *World Revolution and Family Patterns*, in who does the buying and the selling.

When children are involved, the premarital bargains become much more complicated. Not only the practical arrangements about where the child shall live and who shall support it, although these decisions can be difficult and often, as I shall show later, come unstuck. It is the emotional bargains that are the toughest. The one with the child must think: will the person I want to marry be good to my child? How will I compensate for the burden of the child that I bring to the marriage? And the prospective stepparent must consider: Is this person worth the strain of the child? What am I expected to give the child in the way of love and attention – and can I?

Probably most parents who are on the brink of marrying again will deny that they insist their new spouse should love their child. But few will deny cherishing the hope. Professor Goode believes that American society expects a stepparent to love the stepchild as much as his or her own child. He sees it as part of the general postwar "love-oriented ideology." In Goode's view, wooing the child is part of the accepted ritual of courting a parent; women especially demand it.

In this bargaining, which may be entirely silent, many stepparents feel that they have no option to refuse closeness to the child: what the child's parent expects must be given, or the marriage will not take place. One stepfather, a corporation lawyer accustomed to cautious speaking, recalls making an extravagant bid in the premarital exchange:

> There was no possibility of having the wife without the children. The thought never entered my mind. It was a package deal. She would never have left those children, and I wouldn't have wanted her to do it. I would not have respected her if she had wanted to. More than that, *I* wanted to care for those children whose father had abandoned them. I wanted to support them. In rash moments, I even said I would *love* those children.

"Of course, I didn't," he said, looking back. "You can't force love." When after the marriage he found himself avoiding the children while they sulked in their new rooms in his house, his wife reproached him in terms that reminded him of his promise. "If you can't be better with the children," she said, "I fear for our marriage."

Many stepparents have secret fears that life with the children will not be pure harmony, but do not say so. One woman who did speak up and refused to have her lover's children live with them after they got married found, to her surprise, that her stubbornness made, rather than wrecked, the marriage. They had all been living together, for the mother and all the mother's relatives had washed their hands of the children, who were in the hard-to-handle age group of nine to thirteen. The crunch came when the couple decided to marry and the man asked the mistress to use her savings toward a mortgage for a home big enough for all of them. She refused and the children became wards of the state. "If he couldn't support them, I wasn't going to," she said, and attributes the soundness of their marriage, which has given the stepchildren a home to visit on weekends, to her hard bargaining.

It is fascinating to listen to stepparents reminisce about their expectations of stepparenthood. A typical reaction, given with the benefit of hindsight, is: "No, I didn't realize what it was going to be like. All you know is that you love the man and want to marry him. You don't think of the rest." After the wedding, they may realize that their partner has visions about a new life together that were not communicated. Jenny, the kind of woman who dares to be bitchy because she knows her husband likes her that way, described the slow realization that her husband expected more than she had intended to give. "Before our marriage, I didn't think enough about it. How naive and stupid I was! My husband definitely expected that we would all be one happy family. But I didn't have much concept of family life. I didn't stop to think about it until I had a baby myself." Yet well before their wedding she began to get clues that she was being drawn into a relationship with his sons. "I felt there was something wrong when Bill made a rush trip to their boarding school in Connecticut a month after we started living together. I found out later that their mother had told the boys I threatened to commit suicide if she didn't give their father a divorce."

Soon after, Jenny found that she was expected to go to the school and meet the boys. "Alex, the older one, was all right, very polite, very reserved. But Joe got sick and had to go to the infirmary. Later he wrote to his father asking if it wasn't illegal for people to sleep together when they were not married." Did she feel stirrings of love for these boys? No. "My whole feeling was being sorry for them."

Wooing the child is a tricky exercise. The suitor or girl friend of a parent is such an ambiguous figure that children often do not know how to react. One sociological study has suggested that the stepfamily makes a better adjustment after the marriage if the children have not known the stepparent in the guise of friend or visitor with no parental role beforehand. Anyway, it is almost impossible to make a deliberate effort to befriend a child without looking scheming or foolish. The lawyer who swore to love his stepchildren recalled ironically how he wooed them: "It makes me laugh now to think about it. I bought the little girl flowers for her bedside. I read to them. Oh, I knew there'd be problems, but I didn't know how many problems."

Part of the stereotype of the wicked stepmother has her pretending to be nice to the children in order to get the man to propose, only to show her true coldness once she becomes his legal wife. And the mother's suitor is a comic character, down on his knees, playing with trains, revealing not that he will be a good stepfather but that he is a powerful rival whom the brats had better watch out for. Even D. H. Lawrence allowed himself to play this role. In 1912, while he was conducting his tempestuous and successful campaign to persuade Frieda Weekley to leave her professor husband and three children in order to come away with him, he cultivated the children. Frieda recalled years later:

> He had taken my two little girls and me for a walk in Sherwood Forest, through some fields we walked, and the children ran all over the place and we came to a brook . . . it ran rather faster under a small stone bridge. The children were thrilled. . . . He made them paper boats and put burning matches into them; "this is the Spanish Armada, and you won't know what that was." "Yes, we do," the older girl said promptly. I can see him now, crouching down, so intent on the game, so young and quick.

Yet once Lawrence had prised Frieda away from her family, he was not interested in being a stepfather; he wanted Frieda to give up being a mother – except to him. Professor Weekley, in any case, refused to let the children see their mother. The result was that during much of her early years with Lawrence, Frieda was lacerated with longing for her children. Lawrence was unsympathetic. Frieda wrote to their friend, the literary critic Edward Garnett: "Over the children, I thought he was beastly; he hated me for being miserable, not a moment of misery did he put up with; he denied all the suffering and suffered all the more, like his mother before him; how we fought over this." Yet somewhere inside himself Lawrence must have sympathized, perhaps even himself longed to see the children again, for in *The Rainbow*, the novel written during his first years with Frieda and published in 1915, he has drawn one of the most tender portraits of a step-father-stepdaughter relationship in all of English literature. It was during those early years, too, that it must have begun to be apparent that he and Frieda would have no children of their own and that, her fertility proved, it was he who was probably sterile.

Some people marry in spite of the stepchildren. Others marry because of them. For many who have not married at the conventional age, the prospect of a ready-made family is an attraction in itself. It provides a chance to draw even with their age group and to pull out of the emotional hope chest all the stored-up feelings that parents are supposed to have. Sometimes these feelings fit the stepchildren who are supposed to wear them, sometimes they do not.

Stepparents have to guard carefully against unrealistic expectations. A psychoanalyst told me of a patient who married a woman with three children in order to compensate for the three children he left behind when he divorced his wife. The man, eager to be a father to them, was devastated to find that they had not the slightest interest in being his children. A stepmother who at the age of thirty-two married a widower with a small daughter told me: "I remember thinking that I would marry him even if I didn't love him because I wanted the child." What she found instead was that she soon had her own children by this man and that she loved them much more than the stepchild, to her intense guilt.

A primary motive of many stepparents is to be reparative. They see a child who has been hurt, and they positively want to do some good. The child seems a bonus. This ambition, generous as it sounds, is itself often unrealistic, for the sheer fact that children have suffered a traumatic loss makes it more difficult for them to accept help, and the new spouse of their parent is often the very last person in the world who will be allowed to provide it. None the less, the motive is a strong one, and probably exists in most stepparents. Two women used the word "missionary" to me to describe their feelings. Neither was the classic full-time stepmother; both felt they had a salvage job to do.

Margaret, for example, was a second stepmother. Her husband had left his first wife and three teen-age children in order to marry his best friend's wife. His children resented the breakup of their home. After a year, the second wife died of cancer. By the time the man married Margaret, his children were numb. "I had a real missionary thing about those children," she said. "I wanted to help them forget that they had been rejected. I wanted to show them that although their father had left them, he hadn't really left them, if you know what I mean. They only came to us for vacations, but I made it a real treat situation – too much. I just wanted to bring love and laughter into their lives as they had had so very little of either."

Of all the women who married in order to be mother rather than wife, the prize must go to Baroness Maria von Trapp, who wove her stepchildren and her own children into *The Sound of Music*. A postulant nun in Austria, she was summoned from the convent to teach the seven motherless children of Baron Georg von Trapp. "There came the day," the Baroness relates in her autobiography, "when Baron von Trapp asked me to stay with him and become the second mother to his children."

> God must have made him word it that way because if he had only asked me to marry him I might not have said yes, because at that time I really and truly was not in love. I liked him but didn't love him. However, I loved the children and so in a way I really married the children.

Why choose a parent?

The cautious person will carefully ask himself or herself just why he wants to marry a parent. It is one thing to warm to the prospect of a ready-made family, but it is quite different, and not uncommon, to be drawn to the parent in the spouse, or even to the child itself. D. H. Lawrence, who got sons and lovers all mixed up, was attracted to the earth mother in Frieda. Yet in the character of Tom Brangwen in *The Rainbow*, he reversed his own experience and gave a picture of a stepfather who finds the child more attractive than the mother:

It was a child with a face like a bud of apple-blossom, and glistening fair hair like thistle-down sticking out in straight, wild, flamy pieces, and very dark eyes. The child clung jealously to her mother's side when he looked at her, staring with resentful black eyes. But the mother glanced at him again, almost vacantly.

There are two other unromantic reasons for marrying a parent. One is that the stepparent couldn't get anybody else. If the marriage hunt does take place in a kind of marketplace, then some buyers are in a stronger position than others. The people who accept a partner with a handicap, such as children or a clubfoot, may feel themselves to be too old, plain, sexually inept, or otherwise undesirable to try for the top of the market.

In primitive societies, where a bride price is paid by the groom, a poor man may settle for a widow, because secondhand wives are cheaper than virgins. A person who has compromised with his ideal, feeling his bargaining power to be weak, is less likely to complain when the marriage is less than perfect.

Penelope could not be classified as a weak bargainer. She is elegant, slim, sexy, an expensive woman in an expensive home. Yet because she requires luxury to feel confident, because she is ashamed of what she sees as her inferior social position and lack of education, she made, for her first marriage, a bad deal. She married a divorced businessman, a cold fish with two young daughters in his custody.

"I was attracted by the job," she said, "and let's face it, by the amount of money available. I suppose I knew I didn't love him when I married him. When we came home after our honeymoon, I said to myself, 'Well, you've made a goddammed mess of your life.' But there were those two little faces at the breakfast table, waiting to be fed and watered, and I devoted myself entirely to them."

Penelope's situation raises another question that prospective stepparents should put to themselves. Am I wanted for myself, or as a substitute parent for the child? Any study of broken families emphasizes how difficult it is for a parent to look after a child alone. Sheer economic necessity is enough to persuade most single mothers to look for a husband. Added to that are the formidable social pressures on any single parent to marry again. Even the divorced husband, supposedly carefree in his bachelor apartment, finds that he wants a woman companion to help him look after and entertain his children when they come to visit. The children can apply pressures of their own, for in spite of the miserable reputation of stepparents, most children like to see their parent with a partner. Anybody marrying a parent, therefore, has to consider that he or she is filling a job vacancy.

Traditionally, two people who both need a mate do not think about love. It is a business proposition, to mutual advantage. Yet such a deal is seen to carry a coy sexuality.

Here is how Carl Sandburg, more poet than historian, imagined, in his biography of Abraham Lincoln, Abe Lincoln's father proposing to the widow Sarah Bush Johnston:

> I have no wife and you no husband. I came a-purpose to marry you. I knowed you from a gal and you knowed me from a boy. I've no time to lose; and if you're willin' let it be done straight off.

Mrs. Johnston apparently was willin', and Sandburg, no Freudian, was able to dramatize the corollary myth, that of the instant mother:

> Abe and Sarah had a nice surprise one morning when four horses and a wagon came into their clearing, and their father jumped off, then Sarah Bush Lincoln, the new wife and mother, then her three children by her first husband, Sarah Elizabeth (13), Matilda (10), and John D. Johnston (1 year old). . . . "Here's your new mammy," his father told Abe as the boy looked up at a strong, large-boned rosy woman, with a kindly face and eyes, a steady voice, steady ways. From the first she was warm and friendly for Abe's hands to touch. And his hands roved with curiosity over a feather pillow and a feather mattress.

In real life, necessity does not always discourage love. A very young second wife explained to me how she had entered her husband's household as a kind of housekeeper. With her, she brought a two-year-old boy from her own failed marriage. "We each had such *needs*," she said. These were so obvious that it was not long before the husband's teen-age children were suggesting,

"Why don't you two marry each other?" Marriage was logical, but the girl gave no thought to it "until suddenly we fell in love."

> I remember exactly when it happened. I fell in love with Victor in October, 1967. We went to meet my mother at the airport – she already knew Victor, of course. And there I was, absolutely radiant in a new skirt and a bright red Jaeger blouse that Victor had bought me, and my face was – just full of love. There was no need to tell my mother. She saw it at once.

Margaret apologized because her story sounded incredible, but it was not. As much as any stepmother I met, she was the kind of rosy new mother that Sandburg imagined for Abe Lincoln, except that she appreciated her own passions as well.

The single parent who shops for a replacement parent for his child is courting disaster. The *Ladies' Home Journal*, a useful indicator of changing styles in family problems, told the sad tale of the father of twelve-year-old Agnes in its "Can This Marriage Be Saved?" series. The man was depressed, trying to think what to give his motherless daughter for her birthday. What he really wanted was a wife, to develop the girl's femininity. On an impulse, he asked a pretty shopkeeper, and:

> She settled on a perfect gift, I thought – a dressing table with a skirt, new draperies, and a new bedspread in a bright teen-age style. All of a sudden I felt that I had everything going for me. I had met the proper stranger in the night who had picked out the proper gift because, as she told me, she had a daughter of her own who was just about Agnes' age.

The marriage was not a success. The stepsisters did not get along (one cut the other's hair off), and the stepmother, it turned out, could barely cope with her own teen-age daughter. Only with thorough family counseling, major changes in attitude and habits, and contact lenses for Agnes, was the marriage saved, as the marriages in this series always seem to be.

Another complication of courting a parent is guilt. For many people their courtship is simultaneous with home-wrecking. "I do feel guilty," said a stepmother who is the kind of second wife of which the world approves: beautiful, bright, a professional colleague of her husband's, replacing a dull, strident, provincial first wife. "You see," she said, "I was the one who made them stepchildren in the first place." Susan, another professional woman in a similar position, was thought by her friends and associates to be far too intellectual to notice that her love affair was taking a father from his children. Here is a memory she drew out of the days before his divorce and their marriage:

> Before Charles and I were married, I was sick in bed one day and his children came bouncing up the stairs, dressed like Indians and going oo-oo-oo or whatever Indians are supposed to do. They had all come to see how Susan was and to wish she was better. Then they trooped out and when I followed, I found the littlest one crumpled on the stairs. "I got left behind," she said. And when they'd gone, I broke down. I said to my friend who was visiting: "*That* is the problem. *That* is what I mind." Charles didn't mind. I did.

Sophisticate that she is, she remains hard on herself and thinks the world is right to disapprove of someone who breaks up a home.

A stepparent who has broken a home feels doubly obligated to try to love the stepchildren, and if he or she cannot, to hide the failure at all costs. The effect that such a sense of responsibility can have on a marriage was described by an intense man with four stepchildren but no children of his own. He spoke rapidly, as if he had not had a chance to put his case before:

> My wife's first marriage didn't break up. I smashed it. I barged in. I saw her at a party one day and I determined that she would leave her husband and marry me. I am the kind of man who gets his way. I don't care what it costs. In the end, we're all six feet under. The children didn't worry me. If she hadn't had the children, she wouldn't have been the same.

As he saw it, his wife was gifted, lovely, and lost, an intelligent girl who had married the wrong man at eighteen and had had a crop of babies, one after the other. He went in and rescued her.

But, looking back, he sees that it was a terrible emotional shock for the children. He is still happily married to the same woman, but wanted to make a careful, flat declaration:

> Our marriage survived *because* of the children. If I have ever thought of walking out and slamming the door, I thought of how it would shatter the children. If they were my own, I might have walked out, at one time or another. But I couldn't put my step-children through that again.

When two parents marry

In one-third of remarriages, both partners have children from a previous marriage, and these seem to produce the stormiest courtships I heard about. Perhaps, parents already, they have no temptation to idealize the other's children. They know what family life is like and sense the violent jealousy and feelings of rejection that their new marriage may stir up in their own children.

A newspaperman told me the story of the courtship that preceded his second marriage. He was divorced, his wife was a widow. Each had two teen-age children. "We were instantly attracted to each other. We got engaged on the third date. And we were *terrified*." Two adults in their mid-thirties, good-looking, sure of themselves, free to marry, terrified? Of what? The children. Looking back, he does not think their fears were exaggerated. "Each child fought it out with us, right down the line. It's a wonder it didn't break us up."

Another father who married a mother said: "My kids have never accepted Lottie." She sensed their rejection even before the marriage. "I don't know," he says, "perhaps I was too pre-occupied with them. I put off getting divorced for years after I knew I didn't love my first wife, just because I was afraid of what it would do to the kids. Then, when Lottie and I got engaged, she resented the fact that I was so wrapped up in them. I remember that we had one hell of a fight about it before we were married. We had gone on a sort of pre-wedding trip to Rio de Janeiro. I had some work to do for the State Department, and there we were, in this exotic place, with that dizzy scenery, and she just yelled at me, 'I'm marrying you. Not your children!' And she stormed off. It's a wonder we ever got married."

Why do people get married with such tensions in the background? Because they are in love, and it is probably pretty intense, especially if one or both have been hurt before. People who have found a second love are glad to have it and are not going to give it up. The presence of problems in the form of children makes the love seem all that more important. For many divorced people today, children are like the parents of the past – the opposition that shows how much the love is worth fighting for. A musician, with some amusement, looked back on his own scandalous courtship when he snatched a young mother, practically fresh from childbirth, away from her husband: "You have to remember that this was a shocking thing back in the 1950's. This was Great Love. All the more so because of the great differences in our ages." (He took the baby, too, with a nurse.)

If the courting couple are not terrified enough themselves about the problems that may lie ahead, the potential stepparent will find that warnings pour in from all sides: "Couldn't you have picked somebody *without* children?" "Funny, I didn't know you *liked* children." My own collection included: "Remember, you've got to make it up to those children" (my mother). "You'll never be able to do it – you're a taker, not a giver" (a former suitor). "I'm afraid she [my stepdaughter] will break you up" (my mother-in-law). "You're taking on a lot" (everybody).

One woman told me that even the man she married, a widower with five children, warned her. "I did it because I wanted to marry Gerry. People told me I didn't know what I was getting in for. Gerry told me I was crazy. He thought I shouldn't do it."

When Margot Tennant accepted a proposal from H. H. Asquith, British Prime Minister from 1908 to 1916, her friends were anxious about the happiness of the five motherless Asquith children. At the age of thirty, Margot Asquith was known for her sharp tongue, arrogance, quick temper, and self-preoccupation. She wrote somewhat irritably in her diary:

No doubt step-relationships should not be taken in hand un-advisedly, lightly or wantonly, but reverently, discreetly and soberly. In every one of the letters congratulating me there had been a note of warning.

Among them was a letter from William Gladstone, the former Prime Minister:

> May 5th, 1894
> You have a great and noble work to perform. It is a work far beyond human strength. May the strength which is more than human be abundantly granted you.

Some people are reluctant to tell their own parents that they intend to marry someone with a child. A doctor gave the news to his parents in stages: "First I broke it to them that she wasn't Jewish. Then I let them know that she was divorced. Then I waited about six months, and told them that she had a child."

One young woman never told her parents at all – she simply sent along a wedding photograph with a picture of herself, her husband, and a teen-age boy. "But they've never asked about him: they are irrational, overprotective. They have this feeling that the only people that count are their own flesh and blood. They even make their daughter-in-law feel like an outsider. They're not going to make him into a grandchild."

Telling the children

How does one tell the children? Some don't. A widow who became the second wife of a widower was reluctant to criticize her new husband, but certain things upset her about her new life with him and his daughter:

> One thing I hold against him, he didn't tell his daughter we were getting married. I told mine. Of course, mine saw him when he came to take me out. Every time I saw him I'd say, "Promise me you'll tell the girl when you go home." But he didn't. Even though his mother kept dropping hints. It was a shock to her when it happened. I hold that against him.

A common ploy for ensuring that the stepchildren do not resent the stepparent is to ask their permission to marry. Psychiatrists advise against it. They say that it places too great a burden on the child and that whom to marry is the parent's business. But the fact is that many people do, and dramatically such a scene is considered cute:

> So when the children were going back to school, the last night, I took them to my room and I said to the children: "The Duke of Bedford asked me to marry him, what do you think?" One said: "Oh, he rides very well. I like him." And another said, "Oh, he's funny," and the third one said: "Does that mean we have to live in England?" And the fourth one said: "Well, if you marry him, marry him for ever." And I said, "Well, I don't want you to give an answer like that. You go to bed and you discuss it between yourselves and before you go back to boarding school, convent, etcetera, you tell me what you think." And it was a unanimous "Yes." So I telephoned my husband – I called him Ian by that time – and I said: "Well, if you still want me, I'll marry you."

> *The Duchess of Bedford, in a television interview.*

In front of the children?

Should the sex life of the unmarried parent be concealed from the children? There is far less consensus on this issue than there is on divorce or premarital intercourse. A child psychiatrist in Manhattan told me that he is often confronted, especially at vacation times, by a parent and lover who do not know what to do. They don't want to be hypocrites or prudes and they don't want to sleep apart for the whole of a Christmas or summer holiday. On the other hand, they know that children do not like to be forcibly reminded of their parents' sexuality (think of your own parents), and they do not want to upset a child already unsettled by a divorce. His advice may not seem very helpful. "I tell them, 'Do what you feel is right,' " he says.

What feels right depends in part – but only in part – on the ages of the children and what they have been taught about sex. Obviously, if they are adolescent and have not been exhorted to remain virgin until marriage, the parent will probably decide that what is permitted the child should be permitted the parent. And if the child has been brought up to remain chaste, the parent will probably want at least to appear to do the same while unmarried. But the conflict is real and deep between those who feel that children should know that the parent is a human being who likes someone to share his bed, regularly or occasionally, and those who feel that bed symbolizes union and that a child can only handle the emotions aroused by the parent's sexuality if he thinks that some kind of permanence is involved.

There is no shortage of adults who expect, almost as a matter of principle, that their very small children acknowledge that the parent's bed partner has nothing to do with the child. A beautiful young woman, with streaming hair and Peruvian poncho, recalled the first time she saw her stepdaughter:

> I met Christopher at a singles' bar. We had met a year before, but he was with another woman and we hadn't particularly noticed each other. But when we met again we recognized each other and began to talk. We spent the night together. When I woke up in the morning, the first thing I noticed was all these women's clothes hanging around, and I said, "My God, where is she?" He said, "Don't worry. She's not here. She never comes here any more." And then he went into the next room and there was this two-year-old. He had been looking after her, you see, all by himself, after the mother walked out. And she sat up, bright as anything, and said, "Who are you?" So we all had breakfast together. I didn't try to help or do anything for her. I tried to stay right out of it.

Somehow her potential for mothering must have made itself known, for she and Christopher have not only married and had children, but her home has become a haven for his children by other wives and liaisons, and his ex-wives and ex-mothers-in-law confide in her as well.

Norman Mailer is of the same school of thought. In *Prisoner of Sex*, he congratulates himself on his maternal skill in presiding over a household containing his five children, whose ages ranged from thirteen to four, and "an old love, his dearest old love" who was invited for the summer. "In a Maine menage, which must have excited some remarkable curiosity from the exterior but was close to reasonable within, he therefore spent six good hard-working mindless weeks with his daughters, his sons, and his mistress, his brain full of menus and shopping lists and projects and outings."

Many people, more orthodox in their habits, none the less abandon the pretence of sleeping separately because it is simply too inconvenient, while others, who consider themselves moral progressives, none the less encase themselves in monastic sleeping bags or tiptoe around in the dark, for the sake of the children's peace of mind.

Dorothy, a second wife in her early thirties, told me of a protracted cautious courtship dominated by the concern about the effect that the marriage would have on the children. She was one of the many stepparents who opened with a statement that she had not wrecked a home. "Sam says that marriages are broken from within," she said. "You can't break up a happy marriage, he says, and I agree." None the less, her husband was still living with his first wife when he met Dorothy at a conference. It was love, instant and mutual, but neither at first gave in to it. They started a correspondence, fitful until Sam wrote: "I've never thought of getting divorced until I met you. Nobody in my family has ever been divorced. But I can't get you out of my mind."

They decided to see each other for a weekend, and only after that, when they were sure they wanted to marry, did Sam leave home. As the next step, Dorothy moved to Sam's city, but they did not live together. She had her apartment, he had his. "We were very straight," Dorothy said. "Our primary concern was with the kids. We had endless discussions about them, and finally we decided that it was best for them that we got married. I saw the kids on outings and things. They were very discreet. They didn't talk to me about their mother and they didn't talk about me to her. They still wanted Daddy to come back to Mommy. They didn't see us in bed together until after the wedding. Then the first weekend they came to stay, all three of them climbed into bed with us."

Sexual standards alter, but what does not is the fact that to see their parent in love makes many people sick. It is a nausea that is not dispelled by age. Hamlet, in his revulsion, combined the thought of the twice-cooked meats (with the suggestion of salmonella poisoning), served both at his father's funeral and his mother's wedding, with his at the "reechy kisses" of middle age. A common solution for grown children is to deny the sexuality of a later marriage: "You cannot call it love, for at your age/The heyday in the blood is tame, it's humble," says Hamlet to his mother. When my grandfather remarried in his sixties, my mother said, in effect, the same thing: "Companionship – that's all he wants. Somebody to make a home for him and she *is* a very good cook." Underneath these statements lies the suspicion (now confirmed by the researches of Masters and Johnson) that even for people in their eighties, something more than food may be wanted from a partner.

In the past, recognition that the parent was interested in sexual intercourse and had married again was likely to have been a double shock. The anguish that a child can feel at such a time is described movingly by D. H. Lawrence in *The Rainbow*:

"*Why* do you sleep with *my* mother? My mother sleeps with me," her voice quivering.

"You come as well, an' sleep with both of us," he coaxed.

"Mother!" she cried, turning, appealing against him.

"But I must have a husband, darling. All women must have a husband."

"And you like to have a father with your mother, don't you?" said Brangwen.

Anna glowered at him. She seemed to cogitate.

"No," she cried fiercely at length, "no, I don't *want*." And slowly her face puckered, she sobbed bitterly.

He stood and watched her, sorry. But there could be no altering it.

Are parents' weddings traumatic for children? The generally accepted view, probably because it is what people want to believe, is that they are not. But they are curious occasions, when grown men and women often pretend that the children can totally put out of their minds thoughts about the parent who is no longer there. Second and subsequent weddings are properly (so the wedding books say) kept small and quiet, but it is both commonplace and socially correct to have a child participate in the remarriage. Jacqueline Kennedy Onassis and Audrey Hepburn, both manner-conscious ladies, had their children by their side when they took new husbands. As long ago as 1922, the first edition of Emily Post's *Etiquette* explained how to have a second wedding with style; it cited the remarriage of a widow "who wore a dress of gray and a Dutch cap of silver lace, and had her little girl in quaint cap and long dress, to match her, as maid of honor."

For all their mixed feelings, and whatever the circumstances, children of any age can be relieved to see their parent happily settled with a mate. "My stepson, who was fourteen then, was really happy about our marriage," a Canadian girl told me. "We were in Colorado skiing, the three of us. We had asked him if he was uncomfortable because we weren't married and he had said no. But when Frank and I made the decision – we were in our room – right away he said, 'I'm going down to tell Mike.' Mike was so sweet. He asked if he could be his father's best man. But he wasn't old enough."

But whose wedding is it? One stepfather, who loved his stepdaughters and intended to adopt them as soon as possible after the wedding, rewrote the words of the wedding ceremony so that the two girls could come forward and be included in a special family blessing. In contrast, two psychiatrists planning their wedding felt they had to discourage the oedipal fantasies of the man's daughter: "It was a Jewish wedding and the child wanted to stand under the wedding arch with us," said her stepmother. "We finally decided that she had to come to terms with the fact that her father was marrying another woman, not her, and so we decided that it was best that she stand back with the guests."

If the child's own parents have parted only recently and the breaking up of the home has been painful, the marrying couple may feel that the wedding is too much for the child to bear. Dorothy, the "straight" stepmother, said:

We played our marriage low-key. The children didn't come. They were not ready to enjoy their Daddy's marriage to another woman.

The divorce had only been final for three weeks. Even now, after four years, the kids are still mourning the breakup. Our happiness – oh, we give them all that. Ours is a model of a good marriage. We want them to see that. But the actual wedding we spared them, and we keep our anniversaries to ourselves.

Yet a marrying parent is a paradoxical figure, and part of the paradox is that the child becomes in some ways like his parent's parent. At our wedding, my stepson was like a little father. When my husband stood on a chair and made a speech, saying how happy we were to be married, my stepson, in his new flannel suit, stood beaming, hands royally behind his back. He helped the bartender and made cheerful conversation with strangers. His whole bearing was mature, warm, and understanding, and it lasted for about three months. Then he crumpled into a state of total war against both of us, me particularly, that lasted for the next ten years.

For my stepdaughter, our wedding was a shock. Every little girl may want to marry Daddy, but not every little girl gets a new dress, new shoes, and flowers in her hair to watch Daddy marry somebody else. She sailed into the registry office like the mother of the bride. She had organized everything. There were enough potato chips, the flowers had come on time; she could enjoy herself. After the ceremony was over, she stumped out, a little girl with a doughface and knee socks that were too tight. "I take thee . . . " She broke off. "I knew all the words," she said bitterly, "and nobody asked me to say anything."

CHAPTER 5

The desolate stepchild

A divorced man, much in love with a friend of mine who was separated from her husband, confessed to me, a stepmother, that there was one big worry. Not her boys, but his girls. "They are terrible to Julia," he said. "They won't speak to her, or if they do, they are rude. If they visit her with me, they complain about the food she cooks for them." His distress was acute, for he loved his daughters, who were just entering adolescence, and he wanted to see them as much as possible. "When will it go away?" he implored. "Will it be better when we're married? How long does this hostility last?"

The fact is that it might not go away. Stepparents are, in a fundamental sense, unwanted parents. Research shows that children do not easily accept substitute parents and that there is more discord and tension in stepfamilies than in ordinary families. None of this travail is inevitable. Many stepparents and stepchildren come to love each other dearly, but the dubious prognosis for steprelations should be faced.

The amount of sociological research that has been done on relations within the stepfamily is pathetically small. I will summarize it anyway, for I know stepparents will seize on any scrap of information that releases them from the subjectivity of their own experience. Perhaps the most comprehensive study so far is that by Charles Bowerman and Donald Irish of the University of North Carolina, published in 1962. After interviewing 2,145 stepchildren of junior and senior high school age in Ohio, North Carolina, and the state of Washington, they decided that the cultural ideal – that the stepparent be like a real parent to the stepchild – was not often achieved. Instead, most of the stepchildren believed that the stepparent was less fair to them than the natural parent, and that stepmothers were less satisfactory approximations of real mothers than stepfathers were of real fathers. Stepchildren often felt more distant from *both* parents, the natural parent as well as the stepparent, than did children living with two of their own parents. Bowerman and Irish concluded that stepchildren suffered from "greater levels of uncertainty of feelings, insecurity of position and strain" than did children in ordinary homes.

In 1966 Irene Fast and Albert Cain of the University of Michigan examined fifty stepchildren brought to a child guidance clinic. Stepfamilies, they found, were particularly vulnerable to stress and breakdown, and "however strong the stepparent's determination to be a substitute parent, however skillful his efforts, he cannot succeed totally." Fast and Cain also agreed that for the stepparent "to enact the role of nonparent is socially disapproved." As stepparents tried, and failed, to strike the right balance between parent and nonparent, they often denied that there were any problems at all. Some were hypersensitive to every event that showed that the child was not really theirs. Many focused on the child as the source of all the tensions within the marriage.

Gloom dominates the scant professional literature on this subject. In a scholarly book on the stepchild that appeared in 1953, William C. Smith, a sociologist, examined twenty-nine studies of juvenile delinquency – British as well as American – which suggested, in sum, that stepchildren have a higher rate of delinquency than those from unbroken homes. A doctoral thesis done in 1943 by Annie White from the Illinois Institute of Juvenile Research traced some of the behavioral disturbances in a group of forty-one stepchildren to the fact that two-thirds of them had been separated from their surviving parent before that parent remarried. Moreover, the stepparents, even more than the parents, identified the child as an obstacle to happiness in the marriage, and often felt that the child was using the cruel stepparent myth against them in complaints to the neighbors.

A small study done in India in 1961 compared twenty-one stepchildren with twenty-one nonstepchildren aged from eleven to sixteen and found the stepchildren more anxious and insecure: "They feel themselves rejected, dejected and depressed." And in

1955 a paper published by Dr. Edward Podolsky, a child psychiatrist at King's County Hospital in Brooklyn, considered the emotional problems of stepchildren and concluded that the stepparent's chances of success, particularly if the stepparent was a woman, were not good. To the children, the stepparent is very much like a new baby, an intruder, and if the stepparent is immature, he or she can demand a disproportionate amount of attention from the spouse so that the children's fears of losing their natural parent may be well-founded.

The disturbance, whatever is the cause, affects the whole stepfamily – parent, stepparent, stepchild, and child of the marriage. Gerda Schulman of the Jewish Family Service in New York City, in a perceptive paper published in 1972, has identified two characteristics that make stepfamilies different from ordinary families. "Fantasies and hopes play larger parts [in the stepfamily] than in ordinary families," while "natural parents seem to have greater ability to deal with their children in a rational way." The whole family suffers from the contradictory myths of the cruel stepparent and of the instant love a stepparent is expected to provide, and, most pernicious, "the stepparent seems to expect from the stepchild more gratitude and acknowledgment," and these are rarely shown.

How true are these findings today, now that there has been a revolution in thinking on sex and divorce? Particularly because they are so recent, the far more cheerful results obtained by Dr. Lucile Duberman of Rutgers University deserve attention. Dr. Duberman, who studied eighty-eight stepfamilies in a suburb of Cleveland in the late 1960's, reported in the *Journal of Marriage and the Family* in May, 1973, that the stepparent-stepchild relationship was "reasonably good." Many of the stepparents she interviewed reported excellent relations with their stepchildren; some got along better with them than they did with their own children.

None the less, along with her predecessors, Dr. Duberman had bad news for stepmothers. They were far less likely than stepfathers to achieve excellent relations with their stepchildren. And if there was trouble, it persisted. While only 1 per cent of the men she interviewed felt that their relations with the stepchildren had grown worse over the years, 12 per cent of the stepmothers reported a deterioration. Moreover, stepbrothers and stepsisters brought together by the marriage of parents often got along poorly. (I was intrigued by one detail in Dr. Duberman's observation of stepsiblings. Relationships were more often described as excellent when all lived in the same house than when siblings lived apart and met on visits.)

At what age can a child most easily accept a stepparent? All agree that adolescence is probably the worst time for a child to become a stepchild. Both very young children and near-adult children make easier adjustments. A common pattern is for children in the family to split up: the young look to the stepparent as a replacement for the lost parent; the older ones, with clearer memories of the real parent, reject the intruder. Yet there is no "best age" because there can be problems from infancy to middle age when the parent remarries. Dr. Duberman quoted a stepfather of older children as saying, "If there were young children involved, I would be very hesitant about it and say 'don't.' " Many stepparents, if given the choice of age of a stepchild, would argue that the older the better, for the older the child, the sooner out of the house. The smaller the child, the more likely he is to rush in and jump on the bed at any hour of day or night.

Social research on this subject is full of apologies, because there is so little of it. The questions about what life in a stepfamily is like seem increasingly so important that it is unsatisfying to professionals to have to present such inconsistent and inconclusive answers. Much remains to be done.

The psychoanalytic view

To psychoanalysts, the stepchild is a child who has tough emotional puzzles to solve. The first is the gratuitous revival of the sexual conflicts in what Freud described as the Oedipus complex. Ordinarily, the desire for the parent of the opposite sex and the rivalry with the parent of the same sex are worked through by the child between the ages of three and five and then again during adolescence. At either stage, when the Oedipal

tensions are strong, the appearance of the new sexual partner
with the parent can easily disturb the child. A boy is reminded
that he is not man enough for his mother, a girl that she is the
inevitable loser in the sexual competition for her father.

In a paper on the psychological problems of stepchildren, the
analyst Dr. Else Heilpern wrote that replacement of a lost
parent by a stepparent may activate the Oedipus complex "in an
eminently negative sense." What Dr. Heilpern saw was the stepchild's forced regression to the helplessness and inferiority of the
infant. To emerge from such a state, a child needs "the presence
of the helping, beloved parents, in the shape of the almighty
consoling power they had assumed in early childhood." But this
help is just what the stepchild, by definition, cannot have. One
parent is not there. As a result, Dr. Heilpern concluded, "the
situation of the stepchild is especially desolate and hopeless."

One of the remedies that she suggested seemed drastic to me –
removing the child from the family, sending him to live with a
relative or to a boarding school. (Isn't this the theme of banishment which appears so often in the fairy tales? Snow White and
Hansel and Gretel were banished to the deep forests, supposedly
to their deaths; Cinderella was kept in the kitchen.) Yet although
expelling a stepchild from the home is hardly a happy solution, it
does often happen. That a sober psychoanalytic scholar should
have recommended it, is, I think, a good measure of the intensity
of primitive feeling of sexual rivalry aroused in both the stepchild
and the stepparent.

Speaking privately to me in London in 1973, Dr. John Bowlby
expressed himself equally bluntly. "There is no doubt about it. A
stepparent is a very unsatisfactory parent for a child to have. It is
nobody's fault. It's a fact. The myth has validity to it." In his
view, the stepparent can never feel the same degree of involve-
ment with a stepchild as with an own child. "The stepparent,"
said Dr. Bowlby, "can always say 'I'm eager to do my best,
but. . . .' "

All analysts emphasize that the hatred felt by stepchildren
toward their stepparents is the same hatred and rivalry that all
children feel for their own parents. But as stepchildren feel that
their hostility has real justification, they find it harder to resolve

it. According to J. C. Fluegel, whose *Psychoanalytic Study of the Family*, written in 1931, rings remarkably true today, the stepparent becomes a natural target:

> A child's feelings of love and hate toward his parents are usually intensely stirred by all manifestations on their part of conjugal unhappiness or infidelity and when barriers which prevent the full expression of these feelings toward the child's real parents are removed by the substitution of a stepparent, this new parent will often receive the full force of the love or hate which had hitherto been pent up.

Psychiatrists talk of the children's concentrated hostility toward a stepparent in terms of the mechanism they call "splitting." That is, when the contradictory feelings of love and hate are divided in the mind and projected onto two different objects or people, one of them is then seen as entirely good and the other as entirely evil. The stepchild enjoys a heaven-sent opportunity for splitting. Unlike the ordinary child, who has to learn to live with the fact that the good mother who comforts him is also the bad mother who punishes him, the stepchild can assign all the good qualities to the real mother and the bad qualities to the stepmother. Or vice versa.

One psychiatrist ventured the idea that stepparents can present the stepchild with the opportunity "to split two ways" – both to the stepparent's disadvantage. The child can idealize the mother or father who has gone, reproaching the stepparent for not being as loving as the real parent. At the same time, the stepchild can form unrealistic hopes of the stepparent's potential for repairing the damage and unhappiness of the past life – and then blame the stepparent for the fact that the new life is no better than the old.

A good description of splitting was given by a young woman, twice-married. Her son and daughter from her first marriage live with her and her new husband. On alternate weekends her children visit their father and his new wife. She wondered aloud, why didn't her children accept their stepfather?

> I think it is the natural instinct of children when the chips are down and the parents are putting the pressure on to think that the

grass is always greener somewhere else. They can always think, "If I lived with my father, things would be better." They have no incentive to work things through with us. When you're a stepparent like my husband is, you have to put up with the fact that there is always this other alternative.

The splitting maneuver presents an easy temptation for the stepparent, too. A psychiatrist in Cambridge, Massachusetts, who sees a lot of stepparents in his practice, said: "When the stepchild accuses the stepparent, saying, 'My real mother or father wouldn't treat me like that,' the stepparent must not take the accusation as referring to reality." We are all ambivalent toward our parents. The stepparent must not allow the child to assign a fantasy role to a real person.

Most children not only feel neglected but like to feel neglected. It is well known that many children indulge in what is called the "foster-child fantasy," in which they believe, sometimes only in a daydreaming way, sometimes quite seriously, that they are adopted, that they are living with strangers while their real (and usually richer and more powerful) parent is living somewhere else. The most famous exponent of this fantasy, it can be argued, was Jesus.

The stepchild does not need to invent imaginary parents to play this wish-game. He plays it with real people. If one of the hardest tasks in reaching emotional maturity is to accept the fact that hate is part of love, then it is true that a stepchild has a harder time growing up than other children do.

Another major psychological problem of the stepchild is incomplete mourning. Freud saw mourning, the act of grieving, as a process in which the love, the memories, and the hopes that had been directed toward the lost person are gradually detached and redirected to living people and real events. Yet mourning is so painful that some child psychiatrists believe that children cannot do it. They often avoid mourning by pretending that their grief doesn't exist and by becoming precociously adult. To an adult, their refusal to mourn may look heartless or as if they simply had not loved the lost person very much.

The chances that stepchildren are suffering from incomplete

mourning are very high. They commonly wear a tough shell. I found, for example, that more stepparents complained to me about the excessive reserve or indifference of their stepchildren than of any other personality trait, except, perhaps, bad table manners. This can make a stepparent feel rejected. "If you asked them whether they wanted strawberries or ice-cream, they'd just say, 'I don't mind, Nell.' And I would yell at them: 'If you don't know your own mind, who the hell does?' And then I'd feel guilty for screaming like a fishwife."

The age at which stepchildren best accept stepparents is bound up with the problem of children's mourning. Dr. Gilbert Kliman of the Center for Preventative Psychiatry in New York holds that preadolescence is the time when mourning is apt to be particularly silent and slow. This protracted, delayed, and avoided mourning is, in Kliman's words, "one cause of the poor acceptance of substitute parents."

If children have difficulty mourning, how long should the parent wait after a death or divorce before remarrying? People who want to wait until "the children are ready" will find no agreement among experts on when that is. Kliman argues that children who have lost a parent through death should be given psychiatric help if possible when the parent wants to remarry, because the parent is ready far sooner than the children. Another child psychiatrist, using the same reasoning, comes up with exactly the opposite advice. "As children do not have the capacity to mourn," he says, "I advise the parent to marry again as soon as he or she wants to, even a few months after a death. The child gains by having a substitute parent of the same sex as the lost parent, and by having normal home life restored."

Too many stepparents, like myself, are relieved when there is no sign of mourning at all and take it as a sign that the child is ready to get on with building a new life. Then they are puzzled when the child lacks enthusiasm. A social worker, who should have known better, described taking her twelve-year-old stepson, who had been motherless for a long time, house-hunting:

When we got married, we made a conscious decision to move out of New York and into the country, even though it made a long commute every day for my husband. My stepson came with us, but whenever we stopped to look at a house, he refused to get out of the car.

Another way to postpone mourning, often used by stepchildren as they leave adolescence, is to marry early. They replace the lost parent with a spouse of their own, often to the bewilderment, and relief, of the parent and stepparent.

Death or divorce?

Is it harder to be a stepparent after a death than after a divorce? Everybody seems to believe that the way the previous marriage ended must be the single most important determinant in stepparent-stepchild relations. With that belief goes the assumption that the stepparent who replaces a dead parent has the easier time.

The opposite seems to be true. Death makes stepparenthood harder. Three of the studies I mentioned earlier discovered that children whose mother or father had died resented their parent's new spouse more than did children who had been through a divorce. Some of the reasons suggested by the researchers sound very plausible to me.

1. The interval between a divorce and a new marriage is shorter, on the average, than the interval between a death and a remarriage. The longer period following a bereavement allows more time for the child to adjust to a life alone with the single parent.

2. A dead parent is more likely to be idealized. The remarriage of a widow or a widower is more likely to seem disloyal to the lost parent than is the remarriage of a divorced person.

3. Children involved in remarriage after divorce tend to be younger than those involved in remarriage after bereavement. Women, in general, divorce at a much younger age than they are widowed, and divorced women are twice as likely as widows to remarry. If it is true that *younger* children accept a stepparent more easily, then the easier adjustment of many stepchildren after a divorce could be explained by the age factor alone.

4. There tend to be fewer children involved when a parent divorces than when a parent dies. When a marriage begins to go sour, most couples stop having babies. But a parent who dies is more likely not only to be older but to have completed his family because the marriage was stable until death intervened. The stepparent who comes in after a death, therefore, is more likely to run into a wall of three or four teen-agers allied against the intruder.

5. Children whose parent has died normally live permanently with the surviving parent. When he or she remarries, they have no alternative home when things get tense.

6. People who divorce want to improve their lives and usually are prepared to change themselves. They may be more flexible, therefore, than widows and widowers who may cling to the past, thereby making the stepparent's adjustment to the stepchildren more difficult.

The irony, therefore, seems to be that the stepparent who is most needed is the one more likely to be rejected.

But these generalizations could not be more tentative. Duberman found, contrary to the experience of the other researchers, that bereaved children adjusted better to stepparents than did children of divorce. Psychiatrists, speaking conversationally, always have a quick answer about whether death or divorce provides the tougher background for the stepparent, and their answers are contradictory. One says, "I think it is harder if the other parent is still alive. You have a serious problem of divided loyalties." Another says, "I think that it is worse if the other parent is dead. The idealization of the dead is so strong."

There is, I can report, one group of people convinced that stepparenthood through death is easier. They are the stepparents by divorce. After talking for an hour, they will release the guilty wish that their spouse's previous mate would disintegrate: "If only Kathryn would die and I had them all to myself – then I could get their loyalty." "What I would like is if their father just disappeared. I have the responsibility and I want what goes with it." "It's a terrible thing to say, but it would be easier if their mother were dead. They would be with us all the time and I would have that sense of direct responsibility which I now lack."

Stepparents by death do not agree. They know that the original parent is never obliterated, and if they have any advantage over the other kind of stepparent, it is that they have given up the wish.

For my part, I think the distinction between death and divorce explains very little. There are a great many natural parents, divorced and alive, who might as well be dead, for all their children ever see or hear of them. And there are a great many parents who die whose marriages would have ended in divorce if they had lived long enough. The sheer fact that a child has lost a parent through death is no guarantee that he did not see a lot of bickering beforehand and even form the guilty wish himself that the parents would split up. Life is not neat.

Problems of adjustment

Along with deeper psychological problems, there are solid everyday reasons why a stepchild may feel miserable.

1. *Loss of the remaining parent.* Even when a stepchild works out a successful accommodation with the stepparent, he has to give up that special closeness that will have grown up with his single parent. People who have children know that if they are alone in the car with the children, they talk to the children, but if the mate is along, they talk to the mate. When a parent remarries, the child loses conversation, companionship, dinners out, card games that he or she would otherwise get. And to a child who has suffered a loss, this intimacy has been particularly precious.

One of the saddest stories I heard was of a little girl whose mother had died and whose father was a German prisoner of war during World War II. She waited, living with her grandmother, for the war to end and Daddy to return. He did. And after a few blissful months with her, he remarried. That kind of broken heart can last a lifetime.

Sometimes even the stepparent can see that the child is not gaining a new parent but losing the old one. A stepmother who thought her husband was too uncommunicative with his two sons said: "I've always felt that Gordon doesn't have a natural relationship with them. He spends too much time with me.

Once I suggested that he take them away on a vacation and he cried."

2. *The interval.* Often a child whose home has been broken up is looked after by a grandmother or an aunt or a series of housekeepers. These have often been overindulgent because they want to comfort the child and because they don't have long-range responsibilities. For many children, the parent's remarriage becomes not the second but the third major emotional adjustment they have had to make.

3. *Divided loyalties.* Stepchildren also have to solve the difficult puzzle of loving two parents of the same sex. It is not easy. Adopted children too often wonder about the feelings they should have toward their unknown natural parents. (An adopted boy I know announced to his mother, after weeks of agonizing, "I've decided I love you both equally – you and my real mother." Considering that the adopted mother had looked after the boy since he was four weeks old, she felt she deserved slightly better than 50 per cent, but she held her tongue.) One stepmother reported that her young stepdaughter, five years old, ran to her one day saying, "Mary, it's all right to love you because I've discovered I can still love Mommy." (A precocious statement, but she was a psychiatrist's child.)

4. *Loss of responsibility.* When the parent remarries, a stepchild gives up the satisfaction of shouldering adult responsibilities. As the sexual implication of these is formidable, psychiatrists say that children are relieved to no longer have to be the man of the house or father's little housekeeper. But the child may be losing a role that is important to him. My own stepson was magnificent in adversity. Our family doctor still tells the story of seeing the small boy struggling to prepare lunch "because somebody has to do it." When I came, he became sulky and withdrawn; he could afford to. He had too much responsibility too soon, but at the time it was rewarding for him. Children do have a fantasy, like the Radlett children in Nancy Mitford's *Pursuit of Love*, of seeing their parents' ship go down, all hands lost, and the reins of the household falling into small but capable hands.

5. *Fear of breaking up the marriage.* One thing that stepchildren know from experience is that marriage is not forever. Once their

parent remarries they will inevitably try to expel the intruder. Yet they fear more than other children would that they will succeed. They may unconsciously blame themselves for the breakup of the first marriage. There are pitiful stories of children who promise to behave if only Daddy and Mommy will call off the divorce. I was surprised at how many stepparents reported that the children almost did break them up, and of course, they sometimes succeed.

One analyst who is also a stepfather described his early months as hell. "They had an absolute unconscious need to get rid of me," he said. He had moved into the house where they had been living with their mother. "They very much wanted a father. But they idealized their father who was dead. There was no way in which I could have measured up."

Because of the array of problems, I think that Else Heilpern is correct when she says that the stepchild is in a situation that is peculiarly desolate. The old social stigma has vanished, now that stepparents are so common and half the children in any classroom have them. But I doubt if the tensions of the stepchild's home life have lessened.

The loneliness of stepchildren struck me as I made my rounds, twice, in particular, when I saw stepchildren coming home from school. The first time was in England on a summer day. A stepmother was talking to me about her life with her husband's three children whose mother had died. We sat in her long green garden while she looked after her two tiny boys. One rode a tricycle. The other was just learning to walk. She chatted eagerly, dashing after the kids, settling a fight, picking them up when they fell, and describing her ambitious plans for altering the garden – new trellises and rockeries and rose beds. Suddenly her youngest stepson, a beautiful, dreamy child of about nine, appeared. He walked over to us slowly, and she tried, she really tried. It had been the last day of school. She asked about his report card and his teacher for next year and where his friends were going. He answered in monosyllables. There was an awkwardness between the two of them, like people thrown together at a party who don't know what to say. Finally she couldn't stand it any longer and said, "Why don't you go and get changed now? I've got a visitor." Saying nothing, he trudged off and into the house.

The other occasion was in New England, in a small academic town on a November afternoon. A woman who had been married twice was speaking about her stepson, her husband's child, when her own son from her first marriage came in the door. He was about ten, dark like his father, who had disappeared after the divorce, as so many do, and he had his father's foreign-sounding name. The house was one of those big New England clapboard houses that have too many windows and smell of apples. Upstairs, another boy, the baby of the new marriage, was sleeping. Her son ignored me and walked straight to his mother, talking in a low voice about what happened at school and what he was going to do that afternoon. The telephone rang. It was the new husband, the boy's stepfather, giving instructions for dinner. He was bringing people home and the wine had to be chilled. All right, she said calmly. She had graying hair and sneakers and was still sexy, although she would not have another baby. Her son stayed close to her while she talked and I could sense the snatched moment, before the baby woke, before the clarinet lesson, before the man whose name matched the architecture came home.

Both boys had the demeanor of stepchildren. They acted like strangers in their own homes. The neglected stepchild of folklore may not exist any more, but the stepchild is still an off-center character on the modern family stage and it is not one of the best parts.

CHAPTER 6

Problems of stepparents

Stepchildren accuse stepparents of favoritism, overstrictness, monopolizing the parent, rejection. What do stepparents say?

Guilty, guilty. Too many stepparents live with an uneasy conscience. Who is there to tell them that wicked thoughts and bad temper are endemic among stepparents and that there is nothing unnatural about them? The natural parent, in contrast, is showered with assurances that it is all right to hate your child. My first baby was born in Manhattan, where my husband and I were working for a year, and my obstetrician passed on to me the accumulated folk wisdom of the Upper East Side. "There will be times during the first three months when you'll want to flush the baby down the toilet. Perfectly normal! We've all been through it!"

He was right, of course, but I wonder what he would have said if I had expressed a similar wish to wash my stepchildren out of sight.

Keeping the lid on feelings

Admitting hostile feelings is not easy. A parent who is the buffer between stepparent and stepchild does not want to hear them. Anyway, stepparents believe that they are supposed to be mustering up love, not hate. So they push the emotions the world doesn't like out of sight. And there they leave them festering until, perhaps, they meet another stepparent. Here is the confession of a most likable man, a loving father, an Irish writer married to an American. I found it shocking, all the more so because I realized it was true for me as well. His stepson was still in high school.

"I cannot bear to touch my stepson," he said. "If we sit beside each other on the sofa, my flesh pulls away. I cringe. With my own children, I'm positively incestuous. I'm always touching them, rumpling their hair, pulling them on to my lap."

He continued: "I've never gone in for any of this American sentimentality of pretending that there must be absolutely no difference between my wife's child and our own together. Her parents insisted on that from the start: 'There must be *no difference.*' Of course there's a difference, and I'm afraid I haven't concealed it. One can't hide one's feelings. It shows in matters of fairness. One would like to be fair and I just am not. The two boys row all the time, and again and again I find myself coming in to protect Oliver (my own). And my wife doesn't compensate by loving her own boy better. She thinks that Oliver is the world."

He mocked his own paternal illusions: "Actually my stepson is brighter and better-looking than my own son. Speaking objectively, I can admit that. But I cannot tell you how that boy irritates me. Friends tell me, 'Richard is awfully fond of you,' and I just don't believe it. I found his diary the other day. He had written, 'I think Daddy' (yes, he calls me Daddy, always has) 'hates me more and more.'"

Here is another classic charge proved. Stepparents are suspected of being avid readers of their stepchildren's private papers. Mine always accused me of it, although I didn't. But I think I know what motivates those who do. They have absolutely no idea of what goes on in their stepchildren's heads. One young stepmother told me of rummaging in the garbage can to find out why her stepson had been so upset by a letter he had from his mother. She found out, too. The mother's letter said that while she missed her boy, she was enjoying her new freedom. The stepmother, defensive, felt her action was justified: she could understand the boy better. Stepparents should not snoop, but when they do you can be sure they are hating themselves at the same time.

Stepparents live in a world of grand emotion. Instead of seeing themselves as a little bit nasty, they then see themselves as operatic villains, then blame the stepchildren for having forced into the open an evil character that, in ordinary circumstances, would never emerge.

Listen to the tale of a social worker who was fed up with

finding her stepson in her apartment when she came home from work. He ostensibly lived with his mother but had a key to his father's place as well, and the stepmother felt her privacy was intruded upon. One day she was especially tired, but she made his dinner. Then:

> My stepson was lying on the floor, watching television. He's only fourteen but he's six feet two. And I became so furious at the thought that not only was he cluttering up my life emotionally but there he was physically, lying on the floor, that I kicked him. Honestly, I could have kicked him until he was dead. And enjoyed it. I felt terrible about it, the destructive force that welled up inside me. I've got ten godchildren, I know lots of my friends' children, I've been a social worker for twenty years, and I've never experienced a desire to hurt a child. The funny thing was that I was on my way to serve his supper – you know, "I've made you this nice dinner because you'll like it," the nice kind of activity that the world sees stepmothers as doing. Wicked? I'll say I feel wicked. You feel wicked because the rest of the world doesn't permit you to have a bad side.

Only as an afterthought did this woman mention that during this outburst, which consisted of one kick, she was wearing only slippers on her feet. She was more concerned with confessing her other wicked fantasies about her husband's children: "Wouldn't it be lovely if they all died in the night? Sometimes I just want to obliterate them."

Without prompting, many stepparents said that they were upset by their own blind rages. One woman said: "My four-year-old stepdaughter makes me angrier than I can ever remember feeling in my life, except with my sister." A stepfather said: "We went sailing and I was so angry with my stepdaughter that I threw her the length of the boat, and she yelled at me, 'Don't you ever do that to me again!'"

In the ordinary routine stepparents manage to keep the lid on their feelings – at a price. They give up the spontaneity of family life. Here is where virtually all stepparents, men and women, by death and divorce, English and American, happy or neurotic, say the same thing: "I don't shout at my stepchildren. I only shout

at people I'm absolutely sure of." "I don't hit my stepchildren –
I clout my own!" "To stepchildren, you can't say as you would
to your own, 'For God's sake, get out of my sight.' They didn't
ask you to be there." "You can tell your children to go to hell.
You can't tell your stepchildren to go to hell."

There is a reason why stepparents can feel almost physically
allergic to the presence of a stepchild, and it is not that stepparents have an overdose of original sin. It is because the stepchild is a constant reminder of the parent's sexual intercourse
with the previous spouse. In many cases, the child is a physical
replica of the last person in the world the stepparent wants to
think about, and from physical resemblance it is just a short step
to see a likeness in character as well. Especially if there has been a
divorce and the new marriage is then built on the legend of how
bad the old one was, the stepchild can come to seem like the
absent spouse in disguise. In one stepfather's words: "Every
time I see his face, he reminds me of his father. A real piglet. The
boy irritates me, and he irritates his mother too." A stepmother
said: "I love the youngest two and the oldest, well, he's on his
own. But the second boy. I've never taken to him. He's most like
his mother."

The comparison between the stepchild and the departed parent,
at the forefront of every stepparent's mind, must never be spoken
aloud. To do so is to hit the child where he is most vulnerable.
But not every stepparent can resist the temptation when the going
gets rough. A secretary said: "The girl and I had a big bust-up.
The older she got, the more insolent she was to her father. I
couldn't put up with it and finally I let her have it. I told her she
was just like her mother. [The mother was in and out of mental
hospitals.] After that she stayed away, and her father didn't see
her for two years."

Who holds the authority?

What causes conflicts is usually a matter of discipline. Should
authority flow from the stepparent directly, or take a detour
through the parent? Again, stepparents often see the alternatives
in extremes, and the professionals disagree among themselves.

One view is that the stepparent should begin as he means to go on, showing the stepchild that in the new household both partners have equal authority. The other view is that the stepparent should approach discipline gradually, giving the natural parent time to relinquish the sole right to control the child. Either way, a stepparent has to face the problem of sharing authority, and it is something that must be done in the fragile early stage of the marriage when the child has an irresistible opportunity to play one off against the other.

In any dispute about the child, of course, the parent can always pull rank. A father interrupts his wife, as she is talking about her stepchildren, saying, "You don't have any information about the children's first five years of life." The stepmother acknowledges, "Well, no, but . . . " "You don't," he insists, and he wins, because he was *there* when they were small and she was not. A middle-aged woman whose husband could not have been more sensitive to her feelings confessed that she had always felt left out. "The boy and his father didn't try to make me feel an outsider, but I did. I envied their closeness." And who is to be the judge of how good a stepparent the stepparent is? The natural parent. The stepparent asks, uncertainly, "How am I doing?" and has to take the parent's answer as gospel.

Stepparents who come to the marriage without children – as most do – suffer from inexperience. They probably have lived in childless circles where people have white rugs, keep glass objects on low shelves, and never walk into the bathroom to find that the toilet has not been flushed. An advertising man told me of his reaction to instant parenthood: "The hardest thing was suddenly to have to cope with noise. I had no idea how much noise three children made. I have a violent temper, and I used to have to go to a room at the top of the house and my wife would try to keep them quiet. The whole thing was a shock to my system. All the stages of children's development which other people go through gradually, for me, were telescoped."

The British writer, Anthony Burgess, vividly described the apprehension that his new four-year-old stepson aroused, "me being fifty and never till now having had any experience of fatherhood, whether true, spiritual, step or foster." Burgess shuddered at "the astonishingly skilful construction of instant squalor where I was used to tidiness and order. There is also the demented creativity: he makes sugar by mixing salt, cigarette ash and sputum . . . Children will find anything they want to find, and getting up in the night for one purpose or another, I have been worried to see a small naked form darting from some forbidden corner back to bed. If a grown woman could make pie-bottoms out of Carlyle's *French Revolution*, a boy of four can reasonably be expected to micturate silently on a near-finished novel, carbon copy and all."

Then there is the lack of privacy. Even if stepchildren appear only on visits, the visits can come at the wrong time. One couple had planned to take a prevacation, to rest up before his boys came for the summer, when they got news that one of the boys – "the only one of the four I can't stand," said the stepmother – got out of school a week ahead of the others. "Bob said, 'Let's take him with us! He'll be lonely sitting around the house all by himself.' I was furious but I gave in. It was like taking a dose of strong medicine. I couldn't do it again."

There are worse situations. "When we got married," said Winifred, who had married a widower, "about a year after their mother died, we had the youngest, Robert, in bed with us for the first six months. He couldn't sleep. He thought crocodiles were nibbling his toes. The next oldest, James, wandered through the house in his sleep. And the girl – she was ten – had to wear protective pads to bed because she wet the bed. And as soon as she stopped wetting the bed, she started to menstruate!"

What is hardest on the marriage, I think, is the lack of privacy in the mind. "The children" are always present. The marriage never has a chance to exist as a concept of just two people – until, of course, the children grow up and the parents are alone at last and, with any luck, still fancy each other.

There is one emotional luxury permitted stepparents. They can like or love their stepchildren unequally. Psychiatrists say that even in the privacy of the consulting room, a natural parent is reluctant to admit a preference for one child over another, even though such preferences are understandable. Not so stepparents. Close the door and they will admit freely that they have favorites.

They tend to prefer the younger ones, and they also cannot help but respond more to the stepchildren whom they can help and who seem to like them. A doctor calmly described his three stepsons to me:

> The second is my favorite. We have a lot in common. The boy had been thought to be not very bright, and now he turns out to have an IQ of 140. He blossomed in the relationship with me. But I don't like the youngest very much. He had the strongest objection to the remarriage. Understandable. He wanted his mother all to himself. Now he can joke about it. "I was pretty awful to Harry at the beginning." But he is not very intelligent, likes only pop music and football – two things I have no interest in whatsoever. He is unlikely to get into college.

Emotional styles vary from one family to another, and the sheer difference can annoy a stepparent considerably. If you have your own children, it is unlikely that their ways will seem foreign to you, even if they get on your nerves. But stepchildren, especially if there is more than one, can make a stepparent feel alien in a household. Margot Asquith confided her views on the Asquiths to her diary (which she later published). They had not been brought up as she was. Notice how she accuses them of "blindness of heart" – the stepparent's complaint of the stepchildren's expressionlessness.

> I do not think if you had ransacked the world you could have found natures so opposite in temper, temperament and outlook as myself and my stepchildren when I first knew them. . . .
> They rarely looked at you and never got up when anyone came into the room. If you had appeared downstairs in a ball-dress or a bathing gown they would never have observed it and would certainly never have commented on it if they had. . . . They were devoted to one another and never quarrelled – they were seldom wild and never naughty. Perfectly self-contained, truthful and deliberate, I never saw them lose themselves in my life and I have hardly ever seen the saint or hero that excited their disinterested emotion.
> When I thought of the storms of revolt, the rage, the despair, the

wild enthusiasms and reckless adventures of our nursery and schoolroom, I was stunned by the steadiness of the Asquith temper.

Let it not be inferred that I am criticizing them as they now are, or that their attitude towards myself was at any time lacking in sympathy. Blindness of heart does not imply hardness, and expression is a matter of temperament or impulse, but it was their attitude towards life that was different from my own. They overvalued brains, which was a strange fault, as they were all remarkably clever.

Then, looking back, Margot Asquith, like many stepparents, finds herself wanting:

We were all wonderfully happy together, but looking back, I think I was far from clever with my stepchildren – and they grew up good and successful independently of me.

Occasionally people come to prefer their stepchildren. They feel that they have a more straightforward relationship with them than with their own children. It can be a matter of matching temperaments or it can be a sign of low self-esteem. Penelope, who took on stepmothering as a way to climb the socioeconomic ladder, said that when her own baby was born, she put the baby in the care of a nurse and devoted herself to her stepdaughters. They were far more interesting; they were older. "I thought I loved them better," she said. "I didn't think I loved my own more. I just knew it upset me if she fell off a horse when it didn't upset me when the others did."

The pressure on a remarriage is tremendous. The world is not so tolerant of third and fourth marriages. If you have had two divorces, it is harder to put the blame on the partner, and the older you are, the harder the chances are of attracting a new spouse. Stepchildren add stress. If sexual inadequacy was the first wife's complaint against her husband, think of his worry when he marries again and the stepchildren enter the house with their stereos. One man told me that the week after his second wedding, while waiting for the stepchildren to arrive from their grandmother's, he suffered a nervous breakdown.

Perhaps stepparents do expect too much gratitude from their

stepchildren. Parents expect it, too, but many are somewhat tempered by the knowledge that they do not feel grateful to their own parents. Anyway, even if a stepparent has a right to it, how would a stepchild show gratitude if he wanted to? Families that have grown over time develop all kinds of informal ways of signaling love, affection, and appreciation. Between stepparent and stepchildren, these worn paths of communication do not exist. There can be just awkwardness and shutting off feeling.

Nothing is simple for the stepparent – not even love for the stepchild. Many stepparents are inhibited by the belief that they have no right to love another person's child. This is an especially difficult problem when the child's parents are divorced and friendly. The child doesn't need a third parent, yet the stepparent may find that parental emotions begin to stir. It can quite take people by surprise, the sudden unsolicited love for the spouse's child. In Tolstoy's *Anna Karenina*, Anna's husband, Alexey Alexandrovitch, has such a feeling for the baby he should have hated – its father was Anna's lover, Count Vronsky:

> But for the little new-born baby he felt a quite peculiar sentiment, not of pity only, but of tenderness. At first, from a feeling of compassion alone, he had been interested in the delicate little creature, who was not his child, and who was cast on one side during her mother's illness, and would certainly have died if he had not troubled about her, and he did not himself observe how fond he became of her. He would go into the nursery several times a day, and sit there for a long while, so that the nurses, who were at first afraid of him, got quite used to his presence. Sometimes for half an hour at a stretch he would sit silently gazing at the saffron-red, downy, wrinkled face of the sleeping baby, watching the movements of the frowning brows, and the fat little hands, with clenched fingers, that rubbed the little eyes and nose. At such moments particularly Alexey Alexandrovitch had a sense of perfect peace and inward harmony, and saw nothing extraordinary in his position, nothing that ought to be changed.

But the position is extraordinary and guilt comes. One analyst was shrewd in putting a label on this fear: "child-stealing." For all that society smiles on adoption and fostering, it still holds a profound sense of children as property. The adult who uses someone else's child for his own emotional purposes may feel that something is wrong.

If any single label suits all the varieties of stepparent, it is "the watched parent." Stepparents feel that the world is watching to see if they will be cruel. They feel that their finest motives may be misinterpreted. In anticipation of criticism, they bend over backward to appear kind. Oversolicitude, Freud observed, comes when there is a predominant feeling of affection and a contrary but unconscious current of hostility. A woman psychoanalyst in Boston, undeterred by Freud, interrupted her practice and went every afternoon to meet her young stepdaughter at school, something she continued until a neighbor told her that the girl was old enough to come home by herself.

Because the stepparent will draw the critics' fire, the real parent may get into the habit of passing over all the unpleasant duties and decisions to the stepparent. Imagine the anxiety of a stepmother whose husband had a retarded daughter with a mental age of five:

> Someday she'll have to go to a home. She was supposed to go when she was eight. Then her mother died so she didn't go. Then she was supposed to go when she was eleven, but that was the year we got married, so she didn't go. Now she's finishing her special school, and my husband knows she'll have to go away but he says to me, "You'll have to do it, Grace." I'll have to write and get the papers and make all the arrangements. And then I'll get all the blame. There will be blame, won't there?

There will. It would be no consolation to her to know that George Washington suffered acutely from the same sense of unfairness. His worries were compounded by the fact that he was legal guardian of Jacky Custis's considerable fortune, and he was watched, literally by the courts. Washington himself considered this fact of public accountability as the primary difference between his role and that of a real father. In a letter to Reverend Boucher, written at Mount Vernon on May 13, 1770, he declared:

A natural parent has only two things principally to consider, the improvement of his son and the finances to do with it: if he fails in the first (not through his own neglect) he laments it as a misfortune; if exceeded in the Second, he endeavors to correct it as an abuse unaccountable to any, and regardless of what the world may say, who do not, cannot suspect him of acting on any other motive than the good of the party; he is to satisfy himself only.

But this is not the case with respect to guardians: they are not only to be actuated by the same motives which govern in the other case, but are to consider in what light their conduct may be viewed by those whom the constitution hath placed as a controulling power over them; because a faupas committed by them often incurs the severest censure, and sometimes punishment; when the intention may be strictly laudable.

Defensive, misunderstood, exploited, querulous, a victim of other people's mistakes or misfortunes: the stepparent sees himself as a stepchild.

Psychiatrists say (they're virtually unanimous on this point, at least) that it is impossible to love a child who is not yours as much as one who is.

How then do stepparents bridge the gap between the ideal and the reality? They pretend. I'm indebted to an old friend, a distinguished journalist, for articulating this truth. His wife's son had always lived with them; the boy's real father was "somewhere."

I was a very bad stepfather. Look at so-and-so. He's the very best. He listens to them, helps them with their homework. I wish I had been better. I could have spent more time with my stepson. I didn't. I had other things on my mind. I could have made him love me, made him think, "Michael is wonderful," and that would have been a splendid thing.

I should have tried harder to love him. No, I don't think I would have succeeded. You can't feign love. But I should have hidden better the lack of love. I feel guilty because I did not love him. Of course, I feel guilt about my own daughter too. Because I'm the kind of chap I am, she's had a hard life. But the guilt for my

CHAPTER 7

Incest

"Lolita, light of my life, fire of my loins. My sin, my soul."

Lolita, 1955

My stepdaughter, he might have added. Humbert Humbert, who loved the twelve-year-old Lolita and who had vigorous sexual intercourse with her at motels across the United States, was her stepfather. True, he exists only in a book, and his love affair with his wife's daughter is a concoction of the author, Vladimir Nabokov. But why was *Lolita* so shocking when it appeared? Was it because the novel was, as some critics declared, cynical, pornographic, and anti-American? Or was it because the relationship smacked of incest and made explicit a common anxiety?

" 'Devoted' Liza Shares Pad with Burton": London *Sunday Express* headline on a story about Elizabeth Taylor's daughter by Mike Todd.

Sexual attraction between stepparents and stepchildren can be a major complication in stepfamilies. Let's be clear. There are not a lot of Lolitas among stepdaughters, nor Humberts among stepfathers, although the records of family courts and social agencies show that they do exist. The real reason why sex becomes an issue is that the incest taboo, the organizing principle of family life, is missing. Nobody in a stepfamily knows what the ground rules are. If it is correct, as Fluegel says, that "the de-erotization of the child's relationship to other members is a primary task of the family," then it is a task that stepfamilies find difficult. More than ordinary families, they are plagued with flirtations, jealousies, fantasies, and arguments, as well as the physical revulsion that some stepparents complain about.

The weakened incest taboo is a blatant unrecognized fact about stepfamilies. Incest may be the last taboo in a permissive society.

No one wants to talk about it, in spite of the current vogue for th word "mother-fucker." It reeks of poor homes, Mosaic law, an nineteenth-century anthropology. It seems to have nothing to d with modern family life. Psychiatrists and sociologists wh specialize in marriage and divorce ignore the sexual tension in th stepfamily. "You will find questions of identity to be far mor important," one child analyst said, almost cross.

I can't understand why they haven't noticed it. *Cosmopolita* has. "As stepchildren grow older, of course, the problem ma not be so much keeping your man's daughter out of *his* bed, a his teen-age son out of *yours*." Stepparent-stepchild love is on of the great dramatic plots: Euripides' *Phaedra*, Verdi's *Do Carlo*, Eugene O'Neill's *Desire Under the Elms*, as well a *Lolita*. Social workers who deal with disorganized families ai aware of it as a problem and so is Margaret Mead. In *Anomali in American Postdivorce Relationships* she identifies the lack of clear-cut incest taboo in stepfamilies as the structural weaknes that it is. She says:

> We rear both men and women to associate certain kinds of fam liarity, in dress, bathing, and relaxation, with carefully define incest taboos in which the biological family and the single hous hold are treated as identical. We provide little protection whe individuals are asked to live in close contact within a single, close household with members of the opposite sex to whom they have i consanguineous relationships. This leads to enormous abuses girls are seduced by stepbrothers and stepfathers, men are seduce by precocious stepdaughters.

Because the taboo is weak, thoughts that are so forbidden as t be unconscious in ordinary families are very near the surface i stepfamilies. I was astonished to find that stepfamilies argue ou loud about sex within the family circle. One day, for instance, was having lunch with a lawyer in Washington. We were talkin about communications satellites when he switched the subject t stepchildren. He and his wife had just been divorced. His step daughter, who had been quite small when he married he mother, was a nubile sixteen when the marriage broke up. Th lawyer blurted out, blushing but indignant: "You canno magine one of the things my wife said to me! One day when we vere having a fight, she said, 'I bet you're just waiting for Anna o get a few years older so that you can go to bed with her!' magine! That shows you how paranoid she had become. To hink that I would want to sleep with her own daughter!' He onceded, 'Anna *is* a good-looking girl now. But I can just magine that if I took her to a restaurant, everybody would be aying, 'Look at that old geezer out with a girl half his age.' "

One stepparent openly expressing a fear of incest appeared in a ase reported in the *American Journal of Psychiatry* in November, 970. A stepmother was tormented by the fear that her husband vould be sexually attracted to his own five-year-old son. She aid she was afraid that "they'll run away for the week-end ogether." The woman was obviously a lunatic and had seen in he stepson a powerful female rival to herself. And the little boy vas no paragon: he spilled ink on the wash, cut up his step-nother's dresses, and defecated in the laundry basket. But I vonder how many ordinary families put fears of incest into vords.

In a sophisticated stepfamily, by contrast, seduction can even >e joked about. One stepfather contributed this morsel of Sunday-:vening dialogue. His stepdaughter, a pretty girl, was brought 1ome by her real father after her weekend visit. The father came n for a chat (it had been a civilized divorce), and the girl was inging the song, "I've Got a Brand New Pair of Roller Skates." The stepfather chimed in with the next line, "I've got a brand 1ew key." The father cut in swiftly. "Oh, no, you don't," he aid to the stepfather.

The issue was no joke to two young stepmothers who told me hat they felt drawn to their stepsons. Both had decided not to nention it to their husbands. In both cases, their feelings were lelicate – a sad kind of love mixed up with the wish for a baby. [do not think either, in fact, had talked about it to anyone >efore. Mary, an open, agreeable young woman, had, before she vas twenty-one, married a much older divorced man who had :hree sons. They now have a baby daughter of their own.

"Conrad was forty-five when I met him," Mary said. "Two of 1is sons were older than I was. The youngest boy was, then, thirteen. In all of them, I saw flashbacks of Conrad, what he must have been like at the different stages of his life before I knew him. They all were great companions for me when I married. We went swimming and mountain climbing. Conrad doesn't like those things. Oh, we all kiss each other. My oldest stepson – if I were alone with him for a week, I'd be crazy about him. And my second stepson is very dashing, very tall. As for the youngest boy . . . well, I became very attached to him. He opened out to me in a marvelous way. When he was sixteen or seventeen, I was his confidante."

Mary then admitted, "I'm most sexually attracted to him, the youngest one, of all. I've traveled with him. I've swum naked with him. To tell the truth, I was quite in love with him about three years ago. I think Conrad knew, but we didn't talk about it. When the boy went off to college, I was low. Very low."

Make no mistake about it, this was a woman happy in her marriage. The incidental love that sprang up was something she was capable of containing and has, in fact, recovered from. It is her own future and the prospect of early widowhood that weigh her down. "I'd love to have another baby," she said. "I'm one of those women who are terribly good at being pregnant and I'm not trained for any job. But Conrad is too old. Of course, he fills my life. He knows everything, can make everything. He is so sure of himself. He is not the slightest bit jealous of his sons' youth and virility. He would never think of a thing like that."

What keeps the sexual weeds down in most stepfamilies is the active sex life of the parent and stepparent. A pediatrician explained to me his conviction that if the sex life is satisfactory, then sexual fantasies about the stepchildren will never arise. His view, indisputable in a way, is also pious. Divorce statistics show that many husbands and wives do not satisfy each other's needs, and when a marriage is shaky, the constant presence around the house of a sexually interesting person of the opposite sex does nothing to stabilize it. A psychoanalyst searching his memory on the subject (virtually all I talked to said that incest was not an issue in step-relations, then settled back to recall one case after another) remembered the following incident in the life of one of his patients: "The patient, a professional man who was unhappily married, found himself alone with his stepdaughter, who was eighteen, while his wife was away. They began by talking about sex, then he exposed himself, then they had intercourse. When the man came to me he was a wreck. 'What in hell has happened to my life?' he cried."

Then, too, sexual tensions can arise from the fact that many adolescent and even preadolescent children are sexually provocative. And it seems evident that there are many happily married, sexually replete men and women whose erotic imaginations are not exhausted by marriage. They have an eye for who is good in bed, and if there is a sexy young person around the house, they pick up the signals.

It is even true, although most people like to deny it, that parents have sexual fantasies about their own children. One analyst told me that men complain to him of being bothered by the presence of their teen-age daughters – "bra-less," he said, pointedly. Another had had patients who complained of becoming impotent when their daughters came home from college. A third amiably offered this nugget of self-analysis: "I am intensely uncomfortable with my own sexy daughter. If alone together, we might have a fight. That's how it would come out."

It is impossible to deny the social ambiguity of the sexual relationship of a stepparent and stepchild of the opposite sex. Inevitably, there will be times when they appear as a couple, and even if there is a wide gap in age, as with Lolita and Humbert, they may need to declare what they are to each other, or to pretend to be what they are not. "When we go skiing," a thirty-five-year-old woman said of herself and her seventeen-year-old stepson, "we go as mother and son. It's simpler."

Remarriage is a middle-aged phenomenon, and a child of the same sex highlights the fact. The fear of comparing poorly with the first bloom of youth affects men as well as women, although women with teen-age daughters probably suffer most. Take one of the most common of all stepparent situations: a divorced woman, with custody of her children, manages against the handicaps of advancing age and her family to attract a new mate. She marries him, brings him home, and there, likely as not, will be a small female, a fresher version of the wife. Stepfathers do notice.

One man, who had watched his stepdaughters grow from charming children into teenage beauties, told me, "Let's face it. In comparison with the girls, Elizabeth looks, well, faded." Another stepfather who always seems to have his hands on his stepdaughter; the paternal arm around the waist takes in the hip as well.

In her study of stepfamilies, Gerda Schulman described the dilemma that the mother's jealousy of her own daughter creates for the stepfathers. He may become overcritical of the girl, in self-defense. Or he may feel himself cornered. He wants to please his wife by showing genuine interest in her daughter, yet he is afraid that such interest might be misinterpreted or that his impulses will not stand the strain of being too close to the girl. The solution in many families is the one mentioned by Else Heilpern: banishment. Mrs. Schulman reported cases in which the mother had expelled her daughter from the house. (Lolita, remember, was packed off to Camp Q by the jealous Charlotte Haze, who wanted Humbert Humbert for herself.)

The remarrying male is not immune from such fears. Men have a habit, as old as time and apparently incurable, of choosing a much younger woman as their second wife. The older the man, the wider the gap between himself and his new bride. The average difference in age between husband and wife at first marriage is about two years. But when a man marries a second time, if his first marriage ended in divorce, his bride is apt to be six years younger (he thirty-six, she thirty), and after widowhood, nearly eight years younger (he fifty-eight, she fifty). Moreover, when a widowed man marries a single woman, the average gap widens to eleven years. The greater the distance in age, of course, the greater the chances that the man will have a son nearer in age to his wife than he is himself. Is it surprising that such a family triangle should capture the attention of Verdi and Eugene O'Neill?

In Verdi's *Don Carlo* King Philip II of Spain is eighteen years older than his third wife, Elisabetta, while she is exactly the same age as her stepson, Don Carlo. The rivalry of father and son for the same woman is all the more bitter because Don Carlo and Elisabetta were already in love when the king decided to marry her himself. In O'Neill's *Desire under the Elms*, old Ephraim Cabot is seventy-five, his son Eben is twenty-five, and the buxom, petulant stepmother, Abbie, is thirty-five. When Abbie has a son a year later, only Ephraim believes that the baby is his. Just as in Chaucer's *Merchant's Tale*, when shriveled old Januarie finds that his young wife, May, is cuckolding him in a pear tree, everybody laughs. The old fool brought it on himself. Old men who marry young girls violate an unwritten law that people feel in their bones almost as much as the incest taboo – that it is unnatural to marry out of one's own generation. The Washington lawyer accused of wanting to bed down with his stepdaughter was most offended at the thought that he would make a fool of himself. As Chaucer declared:

> When tendre youth hath wedded stoupyng age
> Ther is such myrthe that it may not be writen.

There are other reasons why the stepparent may be tempted. The stepchild may possess the same kind of attractiveness as the parent. To love one is to love the other. In the reversed-image world of *Lolita*, the stepfather can only make love to Charlotte Haze by imagining that she is her daughter: "We had highballs before turning in, and with their help, I would manage to evoke the child while caressing the mother. . . . I kept telling myself, as I wielded my brand-new, large-as-life wife, that biologically this was the nearest I could get to Lolita."

Humbert Humbert has an unreal psychotic quality because he is unrepentant. He prefers the ivory-smooth flesh of the nymphet to the "noble nipple and massive thigh" of the premenopausal mom. In *Phaedra*, the same phenomenon, seeing the child in the parent, drives the stepmother mad. In Racine's version of Euripides' drama, as soon as Phaedra realizes she is burning with passion for Hippolytus, her husband's son, she pretends that she is a wicked stepmother and demands his banishment. But to no avail.

> I shunned him everywhere. O crowning woe!
> I found him mirrored in his father's face.

Demographic evidence shows that the elements for such triangles exist in thousands of homes. I was invited into one where the new wife, Barbara, was equidistant in age from both father and son. Her husband was forty-eight, she was thirty-two, her stepson was sixteen. Barbara was one of those women who had not expected to be a full-time stepmother. Her stepson had moved in with them – temporarily, he said. She had some objections, yet at the same time she was pleased with the way the three of them had turned into a spirited, affectionate family unit.

"We are all touchers," she said proudly. "We hug and feel and kiss. Oh sure, the kid and I are that way. He'll imitate animals. He'll quack and I'll quack back. We end up kissing. We wrestle a lot. I think it's a good way to get rid of aggression and sexuality."

A high school teacher before her marriage, Barbara understood how teen-age boys react to older women. "They get crushes on you. With most of them, it lasts a couple of weeks. With my stepson, it lasted longer. I feel I can't discuss it with my husband. He might not be aware." She was aware of something else, though. "The fact that the kid sleeps in the next room inhibits me sexually. We like afternoon lovemaking, Ralph and I, and we can't do that while he's living with us."

This stepmother-stepson relationship had an intriguing texture that I don't think is present in ordinary family life. Her account of a walk in the park with her stepson was delivered in a soft, breathy voice, as if it were a very special story:

It was such a beautiful evening. My husband had brought some papers home from the office and he didn't want to stop so he said, "You two go." It was at a time when the boy was being very hostile to me. But as we walked in the park, he pointed out this bird and that animal. He knows so much and I know nothing about animals. It was wonderful. Sometimes he put his hand on my shoulder and directed me where to look. "There!" At a bird. He was just like an adult. I loved it, and he loved it.

But, but, but. However close in age the stepson and stepmother, the Oedipal thread in their relationship remains. She is his father's wife, and, in consequence, something more. An

English publisher told me a marvelous story about a friend he knew as an undergraduate at Cambridge. "This chap's father had married a young woman, a truly delectable thing. She used to come and visit him at college. The father was a busy man and was not paying very much attention to what was going on and the relationship between my friend and his stepmother blossomed. Did he sleep with her? I should think *so!* They used to spend hours in his rooms. Oh, and they had a joke between them which used to amuse him very much. He called her Mummy."

But is it incest? Well, no, not in law – except in a few places. Alabama, Georgia, Mississippi, and France, consider sexual relationships between stepparent and stepchildren incestuous. Most American States, England, Wales, Sweden, and most of Europe do not. If the child is over the age of consent, then the act is merely adultery, and if the stepchild is a minor, then it is child abuse. Incest, as a criminal offense, is generally confined to a person's immediate blood relatives.

The liberal attitude on incest is illustrated by modern English law, which most modern American statutes resemble. It defines incest very narrowly: "A man may not have sexual intercourse with a woman whom he knows to be his mother, sister, grandmother, or daughter." Similarly, a woman may not have intercourse with her father, brother, grandfather, or son. Half brothers and half sisters, for purposes of law, count as blood relatives.

Until it reformed its laws in 1970, the Federal Republic of Germany took a hard line on incest. Drawing on the old Prussian legal code of 1851, it provided prison sentences for the crime, and although it distinguished between "true incest" among blood relatives and "not true incest" among relatives by marriage, it none the less punished sexual union among certain affinal relatives, including stepparents and stepchildren, with two years' imprisonment.

In the United States and England, specialists in family law are uncomfortable talking about incest, for the tendency in modern statutes has been to reduce the number of relationships considered incestuous. Some legal experts hold that even the barest minimum of laws prohibiting incest are pointless and that incest is a symptom of family breakdown, not properly dealt with by the courts.

Sexual intercourse is one thing, marriage another. In many of the places that do not consider the relationship incestuous, stepparents are forbidden to contract marriages with their stepchildren. The marriage is banned as socially undesirable. You may not marry your stepfather or stepmother in Connecticut, Iowa, Maine, Maryland, Massachusetts, Michigan, New Hampshire, Oklahoma, Pennsylvania, Rhode Island, South Carolina, South Dakota, Tennessee, Texas, Vermont, Virginia, or the District of Columbia, as well as in the Southern states where it is incestuous. You may not marry your stepparent in England or Wales, Norway, Germany, or France.* And if you do so in Georgia or Mississippi, you can be arrested on a charge of incest and punished with one to three years in prison.

Why some places and not others? There seems to be no obvious geographic consistency even within the United States, apart from New England and part of the Deep South.

The random scattering of this cultural trait across the United States was noticed by the distinguished anthropologist A. L. Kroeber, in the 1930's. Kroeber undertook an investigation into the practise of what he called "stepdaughter marriage" among the Indian tribes in Western North America at that time. The Navaho, Kroeber knew, allowed a man to take, as a second living wife, his wife's daughter by a previous husband. In his study (financed, partially, by the Works Progress Administration) Kroeber wanted to find out how widespread the custom was among other tribes. And what he did discover puzzled him. About 5 per cent of the tribes actively encouraged stepdaughter marriage, another 25 per cent tolerated it (one group allowed men to marry their stepdaughters only if the girl's mother had died). However, the great majority positively forbade it. And there was no geographic pattern among the tribes: those who abhorred it lived next to tribes that advocated it.

* In some states and countries the law provides for the granting of special permission to marry within the prohibited relationships. There is no such permission in English law, however.

For comparison, Kroeber took a look at the laws on step-daughter marriage for the then forty-eight states. He found the same patchiness. There were twenty-four states that allowed it, twenty-two that forbade it, and two that permitted marriage – but not sexual intercourse outside of marriage – with the stepdaughter.

As far as the Indians were concerned, Kroeber concluded that "it is as if the natives of Western North America had been unable to make up their minds on the point. In general, they were averse, but with no great decisiveness." The determining factor, he thought, must be the strength of each tribe's interpretation of the taboo on marriage with blood relatives. If they believed that the incest taboo extended to relatives by marriage, they tended to disapprove of stepdaughter marriage. If they thought it was confined to blood relatives, they allowed it.

Kroeber implied a similar explanation for the variegated pattern among state laws. In the East and the South, where religious teaching had influenced civil law, the ban on marriage was extended to affinal as well as to consanguineous relations. But in the Western states, with laws that have been relatively recently formulated, there was no attempt to institutionalize religion into civil law and the ban is absent.

It is clear that to either the sophisticated or the primitive mind the taboo on sexual relations between stepfather and stepdaughter is nothing like as fierce as that on father-daughter incest. The latter is forbidden in virtually every known society and is regarded with that special horror that is the identifying mark of incest. Yet there are obviously times when society finds it convenient, in order to discourage stepfather-stepdaughter sex, to treat it too as incestuous and horrifying.

In academic references to incest, father-daughter and step-father-stepdaughter relations are frequently classified together. A paper published by the Judge Baker Guidance Center in Boston in 1954, for example, claimed to describe eleven instances of overt "consummated incest between fathers and daughters." Yet of the fourteen men involved (some of the girls had been involved with more than one male), only five were natural fathers. Four were stepfathers, or seemed to be (they had disappeared). The rest were assorted male relatives. The fact that blood and nonblood male relations were lumped together was excused with the blithe footnote: "Hereafter when we refer to the male figure involved we will call him 'father.' "

The former West German view that a stepfather and a father could be equally guilty of incest sent a lot of stepfathers before the courts. In *Incest*, a book analysing seventy-eight of these cases, Dr. Herbert Maisch found that thirty-two of the men were not natural fathers but stepfathers. As in the Boston study, therefore, stepfathers accounted for a high percentage of the total.

As most girls live with fathers and not stepfathers, it does seem as if the taboo is demonstrably weaker for stepfathers. What Margaret Mead and *Lolita* suggest is probably true. Step-daughters are girls at risk.

Lolita, to judge from Maisch's book, was a statistically accurate portrait of the kind of girl who gets herself seduced by her mother's mate. The average age for the girls involved in the German cases was not the mid- or late teens, as you might think, but 12·3 years – a few months younger, in fact, than Lolita. The average age for the man was around forty, the time in life when men begin to worry about losing their ability to attract women. What stimulated them to action, Dr. Maisch says, was the first appearance of sexuality in the girl – the budding breasts, particularly – and they were further goaded by two circumstances beyond their control. One was the connivance of the mother (this has been widely noticed in incest cases). She threw the man and her daughter together, put them to sleep in the same room, or stayed away from home a great deal. The other was the deliberate seductiveness of the child. There are stepfathers in the Maisch study who could honestly say, with Humbert Humbert, "I am going to tell you something very strange: it was she who seduced me."

It is easy to say that society should make up its mind about incest and step-relations. But how can it, when no one yet understands what the incest taboo is and why it is universal?

The best-known theories, I was startled to be informed, are all discredited. The taboo cannot be *instinctive*, for it is broken often enough in reality, and besides, it varies wildly from place to place. (True, sexual relations between husband, wife, and their mutual children are on every society's black list, but there the unanimity ends.) Westermarck's *aversion* theory holds that revulsion to sex with members of the family springs from familiarity. This theory has a lot of appeal to common sense, for most people cannot begin to find their parents or their siblings sexy: they cannot, to tell the truth, see what other people see in them. But the aversion theory does not explain why the taboo is violated nor why it should apply, as it does, to brothers and sisters who are brought up separately from each other.

Among explanations for the incest taboo, the running favorite for years has been that of hereditary degeneration. This supposes that sexual relations between blood relatives produce defective children, with harelips, albino pigmentation, and dull brains. Much of the existing law against incest is based on this belief; it is the reason why New York State, for instance, considers incest a crime. Yet there seems to be no biological evidence for it. While it is true that inbreeding can bring out recessive genes, these genes as often as not carry desirable characteristics – intelligence as well as idiocy. Anyway, the demolishing question goes, how could savage societies, all of which have elaborate taboos on who may not marry whom, base these rules on a wish to avoid genetic damage? Some of these tribes did not even know that copulation causes pregnancy. Moreover, many of the strictest taboos, including some of those of the Christian church, concern relatives, such as mother-in-law and son-in-law, who are unlikely to form a breeding pair.

How then to explain the special horror that attaches to incest? Why does every society go to the bother of banning something that no one wants to do? Freud's answer seems to be widely accepted: the revulsion at incest conceals the suppressed incestuous desire for the parent or sibling of the opposite sex. The fact that the taboo on sex within the nuclear family is so universal proves, according to this argument, the underlying desire.

As a mystery to be solved, scholars have lost interest in incest. They have given up looking for the cause and ask instead what function the taboos serve. And they have come up with an answer.

The taboo keeps peace within the family, moves the children out of the nest, and strengthens the family by marriages that make new social, economic, and, in much of history, military alliances. There is still some dispute about which comes first: the incest taboo (you can't marry your mother or sister) or the command to exogamy (you must marry outside the family). But the consensus is that exogamy is good for you.

For Western society stepparent-stepchild marriage has been part of a persistent, larger question: how far outside the nuclear family should people be forced to go to choose a mate? Under Mosaic law, based on the decrees of Leviticus in the Old Testament, the ban on marriage with affinal relatives was harsh and extensive. Until the late Middle Ages the Christian Church followed the Mosaic tradition, extending the forbidden relationships to seven degrees of kindred. But dispensations were freely granted, and as divorce was not allowed, annulments for affinity and consanguinity were a popular way to get out of an unhappy marriage. In successive reforms of its canon law, the Roman Catholic Church drew closer to the practice of Roman law and reduced its list of prohibited marriages to those within the third degree of kindred (children of second cousins may not marry).

As a general rule in all societies, the taboo on marriage with relatives generally weakens with distance from the nuclear family. The trouble comes with certain kinds of affinal relatives – not only stepparents but brothers-in-law and sisters-in-law – who are centrally placed and whose ages are such that they may well become romantically attracted to affinal relatives within the family circle. It is odd that the possibility of brother-in-law and sister-in-law marriage has been so often analyzed, while the stepparent-stepchild combination has been ignored.

Historically, the concept of affinity has grown out of the religious belief that upon marriage husband and wife become one flesh and blood. Hence, all their relatives become the blood relatives of each other, and therefore any sexual relationship between them would be incestuous. This doctrine was well known to Shakespeare's audiences and they understood, without footnotes, why Hamlet saw his mother's remarriage as incestuous.

> Married with my uncle,
> My father's brother, but no more like my father
> Than I to Hercules . . . O most wicked speed, to post
> With such dexterity to incestuous sheets!

There is a social function to a ban on such marriages, which is now widely understood, even if it is smiled at. That is to keep one brother from lusting after another's wife and perhaps even murdering him to get her (as in *Hamlet*). It took a long time, therefore, for the English Parliament to end the wavering mocked by Gilbert and Sullivan in *Iolanthe*:

> You shall prick that annual blister.
> Marriage with deceased wife's sister.

Parliament did not pass the Deceased Wife's Sister's Bill until 1907 or the Deceased Brother's Widow's Bill until 1921. The United States pricked the blister much earlier, presumably as much out of necessity as freethinking. Women were scarce in the Colonies. The last state to ban marriage with the deceased wife's sister was Connecticut, which abolished it in 1793.

But the uneasiness remains. The Roman Catholic Church, the Church of England, and orthodox Judaism still ban many kinds of affinal marriage. The Church of England dropped the deceased wife's sister in 1946 and the relationship is now missing from its Table of Kindred and Affinity, which lists prohibited marriages. All ban stepparent-stepchild marriage. The Catholic Church even forbids marriage between godparent and godchild and also even between godparent and godchild's subsequently born sisters or brothers.

Among the various American states, each has its own list of prohibited marriages. Some ban uncle-niece and aunt-nephew combinations. All ban grandparent-grandchild marriage, and a number forbid marriage between first cousins. While most states permit cousins to marry, many people regard it as peculiar. (I can still remember the look on my mother's face when she told me that Franklin and Eleanor Roosevelt were cousins although they were, in fact, only distantly related.)

Stepbrothers and stepsisters, on the other hand, may marry.

There is no impediment to their union either in civil or religious law, except in France, where they need the permission of the president of the Republic to marry. The reason is this. Canon law holds that "affinity does not beget affinity." A man may not marry his wife's daughter because they are related, but his son can, since the father's relationship to the girl is not carried through to the son. Under Mosaic law affinity *did* beget affinity, and a man could not marry his stepsister, nor his stepdaughter's daughter.

Brother-sister sexual relations, it is worth noting, are almost universally less taboo than parent-child incest. Certain societies such as ancient Egypt encouraged brother-sister marriage, at least within the ruling dynasty. There are obvious advantages: such a marriage keeps power, wealth, and property within one family. It seems likely that some of these marriages were made between half brothers and half sisters, who had only a father in common.

In the current interest in "combination" or "blended" families created by remarriage, the possibility of stepbrother-stepsister liaison is usually ignored. But it does happen. I spoke with two people from families where love had blossomed within the ranks. They were very clear that it was not incest. They hastened to tell me so. But they would have preferred that it hadn't happened.

In one case, the stepbrother and stepsister had actually gotten married. The brother of the bride, the stepbrother of the groom, described to me the families' reaction: "Not so much guilt as regret. We had this feeling that they had not been adventurous enough, that they should have looked around more, gotten farther away from home and met more people before they decided on each other." They had, in other words, disobeyed the command to exogamy.

The other passionate attachment I heard about shook the family considerably. It was described to me by the boy's father, a mild-mannered professor at an upstate branch of New York University. "Oh, there's something I forgot to tell you," he said at the end of a long recital of the problems he and his wife had in combining their respective children, including five teen-agers.

His own still lived with their mother, but in the same town, and they visit him frequently. "My son and my wife's daughter are in love. It happened when he was seventeen and she was fifteen. It drove my wife into a frenzy at first but it's gone on a couple of years now."

The professor dismissed any suggestion that the love was illicit. "Of course it's not incest. They're not related. I don't know whether I'd mind if they married or not. If in a few years, they were still in love, I probably wouldn't object. But if they wanted to marry now, it would look to me as if they were just imitating their mother and me – you know, my son transferring his desire for my wife to her daughter. The one whom it really upsets, however, is my wife's older daughter. She told me, 'If you were a real *man*, you'd horsewhip that boy.'" Do they sleep together? "I assume they do; my wife assumes they don't. Most of the time, we don't think about it. We – Marion and I – went out to Aspen last summer and left all five of the kids, hers and mine, in our house together. It never occurred to me to wonder what the neighbors might think."

The possibility of such stepbrother-stepsister liaisons is one of the consequences of divorce and remarriage that modern society prefers to ignore. Stepbrothers and stepsisters, therefore, are free of any ban. But, looking at the laws more closely, what could be more nonsensical than a law forbidding marriage with a stepmother or stepdaughter? How can a man marry his stepmother? It is a contradiction in terms. If she is by definition his father's wife, then she is a married woman and not available for marriage. Yet if her husband dies, or if they get a divorce, she is no longer married and no longer a stepmother. Or is she still?

Here is another fundamental question that our remarrying society does not ask. More than half a million people a year marry a parent without knowing whether they are entering a lifelong affinal relationship with the parent's children, or whether they are entering a temporary mode of kinship that will end if the marriage ends.

The answer, once again, depends on where you live. In some states that ban stepparent-stepchild marriage, the underlying principle is that the affinity created by a marriage does not cease at the end of that marriage. This principle often does not hold up when challenged in court. In six states where such cases were brought, the courts have ruled that the step-relationship ends when the marriage ends. Sometimes it is held that the affinity is terminated if the parent who created it is dead, but not if he is merely divorced. Or it can be held that the affinity disappears if there have been no children of the marriage. A decision in Alabama in 1934, for example, ruled that as a stepmother's marriage to her stepson's father had been childless, the affinal relationship ended when the father died, and that therefore the marriage of the stepmother with the stepson did not violate the incest statute.

In England, the affinity survives the marriage. "Once a stepmother, always a stepmother," a divorcing woman was warned by her solicitor. In England, moreover, a stepfather may be liable to support his ex-wife's child if, while they were married, he treated the child as one of his family.

In general, American law holds that the relationship between stepparent and stepchild is voluntary and may be terminated at any time. But it will not, in many places, terminate the ban on marriage between stepparent and stepchild, and this fact is what gives the relationship that worrying vagueness that can trouble the stepparent, especially if the natural parent should die. In *Lolita*, for example, Humbert Humbert could not find out whether, after his wife's convenient fatal accident, he was Lolita's next of kin or simply her ex-stepfather, no relation at all.

The conflict over whether affinity survives marriage is ancient. The plot of *Phaedra* turns on it. Phaedra felt she was guilty of incest because she was in love with her husband's handsome son. About to die from suppressed passion, Phaedra confesses to her maid that she loves Hippolytus, and the maid, recognizing it as incestuous, is properly horrified. But then the maid hears the news that Phaedra's husband, Theseus, has been killed. Everything is all right, she delightedly announces to Phaedra: it is no longer incest.

> Live then, no longer tortured by reproach.
> Your love becomes like any other love.

> Theseus, in dying, has dissolved the bonds
> Which made your love a crime to be abhorred.

Then comes the bad news. "The King we thought was dead will soon be here." Theseus lives. It is incest once more. Phaedra, full of self-hate, becomes a truly wicked stepmother. She plots to send Hippolytus to his death and takes a poison slow-acting enough to allow her to confess to her husband:

> Each moment's precious. Listen. It was I,
> Theseus, who on your virtuous, filial son
> Made bold to cast a lewd, incestuous eye.

She dies, having pronounced herself guilty of incest, even though there was no sexual act between them and public opinion – to judge from the maid's reassuring outburst – held that the affinity between stepmother and stepson ended with the death of the father.

Today, there are two trends in conflict. Modern statutes quite generally disregard affinity as an impediment to marriage, and ordinary people, Catholics excepted, fervently believe that when a marriage is over, it is over. Therefore, the ban on stepparent-stepchild marriage will tend to disappear. On the other hand, there is increasing knowledge of and sympathy for the emotional needs of the child. This has created a wave of distinguished opinion – Margaret Mead's is a good example – which holds that the sanctions against sex in family relationships must be incorporated into stepfamilies if children are to live securely in their homes. This need to regularize erotic relationships within the family has been cited as one of the arguments in favor of stepparents' adopting their stepchildren. For this reason, in his widely used textbook on family law, *Law of Domestic Relations*, Homer Clark argues for a continuation of the legal ban on stepparent-stepchild marriage:

> Stepchildren and adopted children should probably be treated like natural children and their marriages to adopted parents or step-parents prohibited, since they are actually members of the nuclear family even though not related by blood. Marriages of this sort are sociologically as objectionable as any marriage of parent and child.

Once again, stepfamilies are urged to pretend that they are like blood-related families, for the good of family harmony. Modern society wants to abandon the old impractical restrictions on affinal marriage, yet it wants the functional comforts of the incest taboo within the family circle.

CHAPTER 8

New babies or no babies?

A childless stepmother, about thirty-three years old, told me: "If I had my own, I'd feel more comfortable about my stepchildren. I'd like to have my own, yes. Michael doesn't particularly want any more, it's something he'll do for me. The stepchildren, when they visit us, ask about a new baby. At the breakfast table, they'll say, 'How much do you really want one?' and 'If you have a baby, you won't have enough time for us.' But I don't seem to be very good at getting pregnant. I've stopped working in order to relax. I'm sure it's psychological."

When I first began talking with other stepparents, I was startled that so many opened with the same lament: it was not the stepchildren that bothered them but the fact that they could not seem to produce children of their own. Then I came to learn that childlessness is common in second marriages. Sometimes it is deliberate: one or both partners in the new marriage have had enough of parenthood. Often, perhaps more often, the infertility is involuntary. The babies just refuse to appear.

It should not be surprising when you consider the facts. First marriages are more fertile than later marriages. The 1970 Census showed that among mothers who had been married twice, 65 per cent of their children had been born in the first marriage. People who remarry are older than those who marry for the first time: the median age for women at first marriage is twenty, for those who remarry after divorce it is twenty-nine years, for those who remarry after widowhood it is forty. The fertility of women begins to drop at thirty, declines sharply after thirty-five, and the period between the end of one marriage and the start of another interrupts a woman's normal production of children. Add to this the heavy cost of starting a second family, and it is clear that second and later marriages stand a high chance of remaining childless. This is true even if it is the first marriage for the wife, if she is in her thirties. The 1970 Census also showed that among the age group of women who were then between thirty-five and forty, only 7 per cent had had no children at all. But those of this age who had recently married for the first time – and whose husband had been married before – showed a rate of childlessness that was more than double, 16 per cent.

A stepparent who has to combine the longing for a child with the presence of a stepchild has a heavy load of frustration to bear. The other partner cannot share it entirely, for he or she already has the satisfaction of having had a child and, besides, doesn't have the stepparent's hypersensitivity to the child's faults.

It is a situation as hard on men as on women. William, an engineer in his early forties, had no children in his first marriage, and he truly doted on his second wife's young son. But they lived in a small apartment, and every night when William was trying to work, the boy bounced a ball up and down the length of the corridor. Adding insult to injury, every Friday night the boy's father turned up, brimming with fertility, to take the boy to spend the weekend with his new wife and their small sons. William took me aside at a dinner party and said: "We've been trying and trying to have one of our own. We've both been checked out and nothing seems to be wrong. But with Patricia now forty-three, it's a race against time." The strain of trying is hard on his wife, too, of course, for she cannot duplicate the feat she performed for her first husband.

In this common predicament, there may lurk in the step-parent's mind the suspicion that the stepchildren themselves may be the cause of the infertility. It is not so much a wicked thought as a magical one. Frustration sends people looking for causes and scapegoats. The French anthropologist Claude Lévi-Strauss describes in *Elementary Structures of Kinship* how in Madagascar when a household is sterile, an incestuous relationship, although unknown, is taken for granted. The theme of stealing away the longed-for child is common in fairy stories, and it is interesting to note that those many wicked stepmothers who banish their stepdaughters rarely seem to have new babies of their own. When stepparents do entertain the suspicion, they cannot dismiss it completely, for the stepchildren may possibly be the reason – because of the financial or emotional strain they represent – that there are no children in the new marriage.

I must confess that although I did not realize it until I heard what other stepparents were saying, there was a time in my life when I thought my own stepchildren had stolen my fertility. Our first baby, a girl, came along more or less as planned, although certainly delayed because of the need to settle the stepchildren down first. The second one, however, refused for years to appear. (I think I wanted a second one because, among a thousand reasons, I wanted to balance the numbers – two on my side, two on theirs.) It was during those same years that my stepson was at the stage of mid-adolescence when many natural, loving, mature parents wish their children were at the other end of the earth. His rebellion, and his litter, dominated the house. Every meal was an ordeal: any request led to a fight. I found it very rough going. Then I did manage to get pregnant, and stay pregnant, for eight months. The baby came early – a boy, small, gray, and silent – and died the same day. The Sunday after it happened, we were having dinner (it is surprising how quickly you can recover from childbirth if you don't have a baby to look after), and there was the usual fight about bare feet, Vietnam, the food. "What's this, fish?" said my stepson, raking the sauce off the veal cacciatore. My husband blew up at him and I stared out at the fog. It took all my will power – I felt myself lifting my mind physically with my two hands – to move away from the insane thought that some kind of malevolent trade-off was at work. This is the boy I have to look after and I'm not allowed to have one of my own.

There are a lot of pressures to produce a child in a new marriage. The couple may be happier than in the first marriage and want to express it through a child. There is a wish to use a child as a kind of emotional cement to make the marriage divorce-proof, even though a child is no guarantee. The biggest increase in divorce rate since 1960 has been among couples with children (with the rate of divorce among those with six or more children showing the sharpest rise of all, 68 per cent). Also, no matter how much attitudes are changing, the belief that marriage and childbearing are associated runs deep. The Roman Catholic Church teaches that a marriage contracted with the intent of remaining childless is invalid. Among the remarried, moreover, according to Jessie Bernard's study, there is a habit of dividing the marriages of a lifetime into major and minor. For some, the major marriage is not necessarily the happiest but the one that has produced the most children. Second and third wives may feel that they have to have a baby in order to achieve central status in their husband's view of his life.

It may sound contradictory, but population experts also say that remarriage stimulates fertility. There is statistical evidence that women try to make up for the fertility lost between marriages, although they do not quite catch up to women who have been continuously married.

This interesting relation between remarriage and fertility has been studied very little. "Why not?" an urbane art dealer wondered aloud. He was still surprised at how many people bearing his name turned up at the dinner table. "Look at me," he said. "Would I have had six children if I hadn't been married twice?"

Taken all together, these statistics and attitudes mean that to be a stepparent, for many people, includes the quiet misery of trying and failing to have a child.

In my mind, there is no doubt that the stepmothers who have no children of their own have the most difficult life of all stepparents. Although the future may see a change of view, there has been a virtual absence of voluntary childlessness among women in the United States since World War II; women may not want three babies any more, but almost all want at least one. How strange it is, therefore, that so many intelligent, attractive, presumably fertile women bargain away the right to have a child in order to get a man to marry them. I heard of women who made this promise, thinking that their husband didn't really mean it. A stepson of twenty-two scoffed at his stepmother (his third – she was twenty-seven) who said she thought his father (who was fifty-three) really wanted another child. "I think," said the stepson to his young stepmother, "that you are deceiving yourself." He was right. The marriage broke up instead.

None of the childless second wives I interviewed had tried to renege on their bargain. But they tended to have an edge to their voices. A woman historian, now divorced, made the agreement sound like a drawing-room comedy:

> When George and I married, he said, "I'm afraid this will have to be a marriage of books, not babies, darling." Oh, he'd have given me a baby, if I had made a big thing of it. But I didn't. We had our work, and he wasn't interested even in the children he had. We had a good marriage, while it lasted. Compatible in every way – intellectually, politically, sexually – you name it. He understood me very well, except that he didn't understand what it was like to be forty-six years old and having a miscarriage! Some women's fertility may disappear with age – mine didn't!

Childless stepmothers may be tempted to turn the stepchild into a facsimile child. Sometimes while they are damping down the maternal urges, they have to watch their stepdaughters' pregnancies and their husbands turn into proud grandfathers. This is not easy, say, for the girl friend from the office who has been made a wife just in time for the menopause. One way they bear it is to deny that they want a child.

Barbara, the thirty-two-year-old stepmother who liked to wrestle with her teen-age stepson, thought it amusing that she and Ralph had bothered to get married at all. She did, however, recognize the force of parental love when she saw it. "It is beautiful to see Ralph and his son together. It is obvious that there is a lot of love there. Ralph treats him as an individual. If he wants to be a bum when he grows up, fine."

Then she said, with little sharp shakes of the head: *"There'll be no children of this marriage.* Even if we wanted some, it would be impossible because Ralph has had one of those va—, vasectomies. He says, 'I feel I've made my contribution.' The kid knows about this, and he has asked, 'Would you two ever adopt?' Ralph said, 'No.'

"Now I'll tell you something," Barbara said. "You probably know what I'm going to say. Well, it's true. Deep down, I would like the boy to be mine. But his first love will always be his mother and that hurts me. I love him, oh yeah. It's deep love. And he loves me. When he goes back home, there'll be a big vacuum. When he goes, I'm going to get a part-time job."

If the thought that Ralph was a selfish bastard occurred to her, she did not say so. It takes a very unusual woman to accept that her husband will not let her have a baby because he wants her to baby him. Another stepmother, Louise, understood the psychological realities all too well.

Louise was a psychologist in her mid-thirties when she met Philip, an administrator for a small charity. His wife had abandoned their three children, and Philip could hardly hold on to his job because of all the chaos at home. Louise, small, intelligent, bristling with energy, took over. She helped Philip apply for a transfer to a branch of his organization in another city. She found herself a job there as well, rented a new apartment for the six of them (Philip's mother was part of the package deal). Somewhere along the line, Louise and Philip got married. Louise settled the children into new schools and apologized to the neighbors when they raced up and down the stairs and wrote on the walls of the elevator. A saint, maybe. But how bitter she is! "Everybody thought I was the children's mother. I was so ashamed."

One day on the way home from work, Louise had a mental breakdown. She couldn't remember where she had come from nor where she was going. After she sat down and had a cup of coffee, the amnesia passed. When she got home, she went to see her doctor, who did not hesitate with his diagnosis: "Throw away the Pill. Get rid of the mother-in-law. Start a family of your own."

Louise realized that she had always wanted a little girl of her own. Brought up by grandparents, rejected by her mother, who had been abandoned by her husband, Louise had been lonely all her life. At last, it seemed to her, she could face up to her desire for a child. But her husband could not. To her shock, he said no. "I can't stand babies," he said. "I don't want any more babies. Look at the three I've got. Isn't that enough?"

That was about eight years ago. Louise is forty-four now. She feels that the issue is closed, but also that she is justified in hating her stepchildren. "Something died in me that day. I was quite prepared to love his children. If my husband had let me have one of my own, I think I'd have been able to love them. I don't enjoy dependency, but if I'd had my own babies, I'd have had to stay home from work, dependent anyway. But it was destroying me – trying to be motherly to them, and I was expected to *enjoy* it."

Deprived of her own, Louise has developed a theory of what people want children for. She sees them as an embodiment of "the past," something to show for all the years of living. "I knew at the time it was his not wanting to share me," she says, "but it is terribly difficult to tolerate your husband's past tramping around with great heavy feet when you've no past of your own."

Why make such a bargain? Because she loves him. "We're happily married. Everybody has to give up something to make a marriage work. Phil gave up his vision that somehow I'd make it come all right for his children. And I had to give up my vision of a little girl of my own. I get along all right with Ellen, his oldest daughter, now – I still can't stand the other two. She and her boy friend are quite amicable with us right now. But if Ellen has a baby, I think I'll drop it out of the window. I just couldn't stand to see my husband with it."

To Louise, stepparenthood is a flimsy substitute for parenthood, extinguished at the end of a marriage. "That is where it can never resemble being a real parent. As a stepmother," she says, "you're dispensable. No matter how much I've given those children all these years, I think if their father died, I could drop in the gutter for all that they would notice."

Without children of their own, stepparents may feel their sexual powers suspect. The other partner's fertility is proven, and while the environmental movement and women's liberation have been vocal about the advantages of childlessness, they have a long way to go before they eliminate the gut feeling that pregnancy is an achievement, that to be barren or sterile is a disaster. Poor George Washington. The Father of his Country did not produce any children to carry on his name. His sterility will be conspicuous throughout history, although it could have been Martha's fault. Perhaps by the time of her remarriage, she had lost her fertility.

The ancient association of paternity with virility may be the reason why childless stepfathers, unlike childless stepmothers, often seem to rejoice in having stepchildren. The wife's children offer cover for the man's infertility. The world (another surprise for me) contains many secret stepfathers: men who go through their married life publicly and apparently guiltlessly passing off their wife's child as their own. The secret is kept from the child, but plenty of other people know – all the aunts, cousins, neighbors, and friends who were around when the mother's marriage broke up or when she had an illegitimate child. It is ironic how tolerant people are of this kind of deception, when everybody seems to agree that the truth must never be kept from an adopted child, for the child is sure to hear it from somebody at school.

No social workers advise the incipient stepfather, and there is, apparently, little in law to ensure that the child eventually finds out the truth. If adopted early in life and the name changed, the child may never find out. President Gerald Ford was brought up by his stepfather, and it is the stepfather's surname that he has carried to the Presidency. Ford's real father disappeared before he was two, and he did not meet him until he was an adult and a stranger introduced himself one day as his father.

One psychiatrist I talked with had himself been brought up by a stepmother who was his aunt, his deceased mother's sister. He knew she was not his real mother, but he felt it would have hurt her terribly if he had ever let her know that he knew. "If the secret could be kept," he said, "I would argue that there is no need to know. It just introduces emotional complications." I can't help but feel that he was wrong, that the truth is always worth having. Pregnancy and childbirth are physical events – they are public knowledge, and the truth is bound to come out. I was worried by the Frenchman who said to me at a cocktail party, jabbing his thumb toward his chest, "*I* am a stepfather." "Oh," I said politely, "and do you get along with your stepson?" "Oh, the boy doesn't know," he said conspiratorially. "We've never told him." But *I* know, I wanted to shout. How do you know that I won't tell him? It does make me wonder afresh what it is that is so terrible about being a stepchild.

The secret stepfather's motives are understandable, if not laudable. He protects the child from a nasty shock. He gets a boost of potency, and an heir as well. It couldn't be put better (if you can bear the ethnic dialogue that used to be considered cute) than in Sidney Howard's play that won that Pulitzer prize in 1926, *They Knew What They Wanted*. Old Tony, a rich Italian winegrower in the Napa Valley, finds a young bride, Amy, through a newspaper advertisement. Tony falls down drunk right after the wedding and is laid up with two broken legs. Soon he learns that Amy has been made pregnant by Joe, the hired man. Amy assumes that Tony will want to send her away. But no:

> TONY: W'at I care w'at evrabody say? We tellin' evrabody he's Tony's baby. Den evrabody say Tony is so goddam young an' strong he's break both his leg' an' havin' baby just da same! . . . Ees good, eh? You don' go with Joe now, Amy? . . . Oh, Amy!

Amy is hesitant, but Tony reminds her that he has a fine house and a lot of money and nobody to leave them to. "Ees for dat I want dis baby, Amy." Amy consents: "You'll stick to this afterwards, won't you, Tony?" and Joe, relieved of paternity, goes off to join the Wobblies.

The physical and emotional risks associated with having children late in reproductive life keep many remarried people from starting a new family. A systems analyst told me he wondered whether they had exaggerated the danger.

"It's the one decision I've always regretted," he said. He and his wife each had teen-age children from previous marriages. "When we married, we had a lot of trouble with our respective children – mine have never accepted Emma – and we felt that having more of our own would dilute the affection available for the existing children. Anyway, Emma was forty then, and her doctor was pretty discouraging when she raised the subject, so we forgot about it. Now it's too late and I see friends of mine with three- and four-year-olds and I envy them."

Another stepfather, a doctor, said that he and his wife would be prepared to take the chances of an abnormal birth, but didn't think it was good for young people to have old parents. "I'm forty-five," he said. "If we had a baby now, I'd be sixty-five when he was twenty." He shook his head with distaste. There is a special poignancy to the childlessness of a late, happy marriage.

The arguments *against* having more children are forceful. There is the sheer cost of a second family. There is the emotional strain of going back to the beginning, the broken nights, the anxiety about baby sitters, the parent-teacher meetings, and the fights about who is to have the car. One of the men who I suspected really wanted to keep his wife for himself explained their decision to remain childless in quite another light. His wife had three children from her first marriage. "Janet felt that *I* didn't want children. But I didn't want them for her sake. My mother wanted us to have some. But I wouldn't want to put her through all that again – and the older my stepchildren grew, the more a new baby would have meant taking away freedom just as she was getting close to it."

Fear of a new baby runs rampant through all members of a stepfamily. The childless stepparent is terrified that he or she may not make a good parent and that there is a lot to be said for keeping the marriage exclusive to two people. For the parent, among the myriad anxieties, there is the worry about being disloyal to the existing children. Leslie Caron, the actress, expressed this well in an interview when she was asked whether she intended having a child by Michael Laughlin, with whom she lived, then married. Her answer:

I have hesitated a long time about having a child with Michael. I feel a strange responsibility toward my son and daughter. You see, on their father's side they now have younger brothers and sisters. Naturally, the new family tends to take precedence, it is only to be expected. Nevertheless, I wanted my children to know that they came first in my life. Divorce is very hard on children; I didn't want to inflict the possible competition of a new brother or sister on them too soon.

Older children may specifically ask their parents to abstain from starting a new family. A businessman who lived in Houston, where the young are not brought up to mince words, told me that although his children and his wife's children did not have a lot in common, "they're all scared that we'll have a new baby. Last Christmas her oldest girl and my oldest son got together and gave us a small bottle full of tiny candies. On the bottle it said, 'Baby Control Pills. Take One Every Day.' "

But new babies can help. They certainly did for us. My stepson, who smiled at none of us, turned out to be the best of us all at making our first baby smile. And when the third one was born – another boy, a healthy one this time – I could honestly say my stepparenthood had ended. I had seen the end coming about six weeks before, when I heaved myself into Euston Station and put my stepson on a train for his university. He had chosen a provincial university, about as far from home as he could get, and driving him to the station was one of the last things I did for him as a stepmother. I bought him some chocolate for the journey, and he bought himself some cigarettes. We watched a girl with a guitar board the train. "I guess I'll go now," he said. "Let us hear from you," I said, and I went home to the two girls.

We did not hear from him, no letters, no telephone calls, until a half hour before the baby was born. My husband was in the delivery room, in the approved modern manner, and the contractions were at the point where there is supposed to be a breathing space between them but there isn't, when a nurse came in and announced that there was someone downstairs who wanted to see my husband. He excused himself, took off his white coat, and came back a few minutes later to announce that it was my stepson who had just happened to be passing the hospital and had dropped in.

When the boy finally did get to see me the next day, he asked the question which had propelled him two hundred miles at the critical moment. "Are you," he said, nodding in the direction of the sleeping baby, "going to give him my room?" It was easy to reassure him that we were not, for I did not dare to play such a stepmotherly trick, and the baby slept in the study for more than a year. While we were exchanging awkward conversation, a nurse came in and said, "I'm looking for your son." "Here he is," I said, indicating my tall visitor. "No," she said impatiently, "I mean your other son. It's time for his bath." "That's funny," I thought in postnatal slow motion. "Yesterday I had no sons. Today I have two."

Now, I would not like to seem to recommend new babies as a

cure-all for the ills of the stepfamily. They are not to everybody's taste, and they are not always achievable. I was skeptical of a succession of articles in the *Ladies' Home Journal* in 1968 that showed, in three out of three cases, how a new baby or plans for one brought happiness to a marriage that stepchildren were wrecking. None the less, other stepparents do remark on the bond that they see between the new children and the stepchildren. "My little boys worship their big sisters." "My daughter loves it when Harold's children come to visit. The hard thing is when they leave." One way stepparents can spoil what can be an unexpectedly good thing is to give the stepchild a lot of babysitting to do.

The Duberman study in Cleveland, however, confirmed that the rapport between the new children and the stepchildren is not just wishful thinking on the parents' part. It found that a child of the current marriage improved relations throughout the family. The specific findings are worth reporting: Where the new marriage remained childless, only 53 per cent of the families classified the relationships among stepparents and stepchildren as "excellent," and a mere 19 per cent gave "excellent" ratings to the relationship between their two sets of children from former marriages. But where there was a new child, 78 per cent ruled the stepparent-stepchild relationship to be excellent, and 44 per cent considered that there were excellent relations between the stepsiblings.

How widespread this phenomenon is, no one can say without more research. Yet there are reasons for thinking that babies do make a positive contribution to stepfamily harmony. Besides being fun, they are a sign to the stepchildren that the new marriage is intended to be permanent. They can provide a common enemy for two sets of stepchildren. Most important of all, they are not step-relations; they are half brothers or half sisters, blood relatives to link the stepchildren with the stepparent.

CHAPTER 9

Ghosts and grandparents, homes and food

As stepparents talk about life at home, most insist on beginning with the story of the parent who isn't there. There is no word for such presences except "ghosts," and the ghosts do not have to be dead. Often what people had to say about their partner's previous partner was so grotesque that I almost laughed, only to remember that such a gothic tale is part of my own family mythology.

Here are some samples of what I heard. For "he" and "she," read ex-husband and ex-wife. "She was hallucinating. They lived in filth." "He was alcoholic, out of the picture for long stretches." "She was into Women's Lib and deteriorating rapidly." "He is in Africa. That is a good thing because he is really psychopathic." "She was grotty. She ran off with an army officer and didn't care whether she ever saw the children again." "He's an embarrassment. Occasionally he turns up and brings his latest girl friend around." "She runs up these fantastic bills and tells the children that he isn't giving her enough to support them." "He was drunk when he died."

The constant repetition of these stories sent me back to *Jane Eyre* and the great scene of the interrupted wedding. A stranger accepts the clergyman's invitation to declare whether any impediment to the marriage exists; he strides forward to say that Rochester is married already. Speechless, the frustrated bigamist leads the wedding party up into the locked tower of Thornfield Hall:

> In the deep shade, at the farther end of the room, a figure ran backwards and forwards. What it was, whether beast or human being, one could not, at first sight, tell. It grovelled, seemingly, on

all-fours; it snatched and growled like some strange wild animal: but it was covered with clothing, and a quantity of dark, grizzled hair, wild as a mane, hid its head and face.

Mr. Rochester then spoke for the divorced and remarried everywhere: "That is *my wife*," he said. "And *this* is what I wish to have," laying his hand on Jane's shoulder.

The fear of the ghost of the past spouse is, for many people, so intense that they take elaborate pains to avoid ever meeting it face to face. Yet they are haunted. Margaret, a chirpy second wife, pleased with her long blonde hair, blue jeans, and capacity to cope with four stepsons every weekend, could talk about nothing but her husband's first wife. Margaret opened defiantly:

My stepchildren's mother is alive and well and living two miles from here. I've never seen her. The first year we were married, I used to go with Nat when he brought the kids back to her on Sunday night, and I'd sit outside in the car, sometimes for an hour. Wasn't I a fool? I used to see Sandra's back, at the window, while she was talking to him. I used to imagine that she was a raving beauty. Oh, I've talked to her on the phone, all right. She told me I was a prostitute and after her husband's money. That's a laugh. If it weren't for her, we'd be rolling in money. Here Nat gives her money for their clothes, and then when they come to us, they're not properly dressed and he has to buy them coats and things. Funny, some friends of my husband's said the other day – see that Modigliani print on the wall? – they said, "Why do you let Nat keep that there? It looks just like Sandra."

Wouldn't it help if she met Sandra? "No, oh, no. She'd just say terrible things and I'd be upset, so what's the point?" Margaret was still limp with relief that the first wife had not turned up for her son's bar mitzvah. The whole evening she and her husband had watched the door in case Sandra rumbled in like the statue in *Don Giovanni*, to spoil the feast.

The power of the first husband bordered on the supernatural in a description given by a stockbroker, who would not dream of confronting the Nemesis in person:

He never visits. He never writes. But he retains a strange hold over them. They're very much like him and they look like him. He is a ne'er-do-well. I have never met him and don't want to meet him. My wife is a delicate thing, a dancer. I don't think I'd like a man who hit her, took her possessions and flung them out of the window.

I have *written* to him. Once he took an apartment near us, at a time when he was making a slight effort to keep up with the children, and he used to bring them home at four in the morning. I wrote suggesting that he get them home earlier or buy them some camp beds. He never answered, but I heard that he was furious.

What stepparents learn is that any marriage that has produced a child is never extinguished. One psychiatrist told me he defines divorce as "marriage carried on by other means, with a bond of hostility replacing the erotic bond."

The bond can stretch beyond the grave. "My wife's first husband is a very live ghost," an editor told me. "We don't keep any photographs of him around – my wife doesn't want them – but his golf clubs are up in the attic somewhere." His stepchildren treat the ghost as present. His stepdaughter wears her father's sweater when she goes on a date.

The stepparent who follows a dead spouse takes care, but often cannot hide a note of reproach: "He was very intellectual. Things of the flesh meant nothing to him." "She was a great duster, my husband's first wife." "He could never hold a job." "She was a sad person; she put off having children."

The ghost is not always a rival and a threat; it can also be an ally. In one way or another, all stepparents have moments of identification with the absent parent of their own sex. Catherine, a teacher who married a widower with a large family was eloquent on the subject: "The children are a little shy of mentioning their mother – as if I might mind. But I encourage them. I say, 'Your mother would be proud of you.' " "Sometimes," Catherine burst out, "I feel as if I'm part of a triangle. That there's three of us – my husband, Edith, and me bringing them up."

"I knew Edith," Catherine continued. "She was nice. I'm sorry that she is dead." A pause. "She was easygoing. I'm not. Nothing bothered her. They're like her. If I'm taking them somewhere at half past nine, I like them to be ready on time. Shoes all polished? Beds made? Then off we go! But they couldn't care less. One of them can't find a shoelace, and they think that ten minutes doesn't make any difference."

The kindest words about ex-spouses seem to come from childless stepmothers. Often they admire the way the woman they have never seen had done her mothering job. "She must be a very nice person or she couldn't have raised such nice kids, not screwed-up. It would be easier if she were awful." "I think I would like her. If I met her as a person with no ties." "She's a superb mother, been father and mother to them all really."

Many spouses and ex-spouses manage to treat each other as no larger than life. The sociologist Paul Bohannan considers that there is a kind of kinship bond formed between those involved in multiple marriages; he calls it a "divorce chain." The stepmother talks to the mother about the clothes needed for a vacation; the new husband takes the ex-husband out to lunch and they discuss the boy's behavior problems and whether he should be allowed to go on a bicycle trip with some school friends. Too many, however, cannot manage this superficial interaction. Deciding when and how to meet the ex-spouse is one of today's most taxing social exercises, one that has opened a whole new area for psychiatric consultation. One psychiatrist was even asked to play Solomon and decide who should visit the child on the one parents' day permitted by Camp Bide-a-Wee during the summer: the father and new wife, or the wife and her lover? He ruled that the wife, lover, and ex-husband should all go. The stepmother should stay home. "My patient was the child," Dr. Bernard Riess explained to Jean Baer in *The Second Wife*. "I wanted to avoid direct confrontation between two sets of people." As everyone knew the father had remarried, "he didn't feel a social pariah without his wife, and Mother felt secure in the company of her boy friend."

Since the beginning of civilization, the problem presented by the dead has been to keep them from interfering with the living. In *Totem and Taboo*, Freud describes widows in some savage tribes who wore a breechcloth at night in case the ghost of their dead husbands entered their tents and tried to have intercourse with them. One solution was appeasement through sacrifice. Another was the invention of heaven – a special place where the dead can live, yet keep out of the way. Divorce presents a more difficult problem, if there are children; the ex-spouse keeps intruding, and alimony is a sacrificial offering that does not always appease.

The task of making peace with the departed, dead or divorced, is hard on the stepparent who never loved them in the first place. Stepparents must accept their partner's version of why the first marriage broke up, yet never shake the stepchild's faith in the absent parent. At the same time, they must suppress their resentment at the respect, fear, or money paid to the ghost.

Grandparents and stepgrandparents

Grandparents are important. No stepparent should underestimate their power to help or obstruct the adjustment of the stepchild to the new marriage. When a marriage breaks up, grandparents become more active than in-laws usually are in the lives of their grandchildren. They may actually care for the child; they may pay some of the bills. In one family I heard of, the grandparents remade their will when one of their daughters was divorced, taking inheritance away from the children with stable marriages and diverting it to the woman who needed it. They reverted to being parents again.

Psychologically, grandparents are unsettled by remarriage. If their son's ex-wife is remarrying, they may panic at the thought of losing their grandchildren and intensify their efforts to remain in touch with the children. To the newly-wed couple, therefore, the paternal grandparents will be a constant representative of the ex-husband. If their own son or daughter remarries, the grandparents will probably be the people who take the coldest look at the prospective stepparent and watch out for signs of cruelty. If they disapprove of the divorce, even a new grandchild may not win them over. A college friend of mine wrote to say that "my husband's parents (now dead) were unrelentingly hostile to his divorce and remarriage, to such a degree that they never accepted our child as a grandchild." And they will find it hard to restrain themselves from letting the stepparent – the stepmother, particularly – know what is best for the child. My own in-laws, let me say, were stellar. They never interfered or even gave advice, but were always ready to help out and provided for my stepchildren and children alike a steady supply of love and home-made birthday cakes. And they appreciated me. "Granny says we should be nice to you," my stepdaughter informed me rather disgustedly when she was small. "She said that if it weren't for you, *we'd* be in a fix."

Never in history have grandparents been so influential in family life. Never before have they lived so long. According to the Metropolitan Life Insurance Company, a white child who was ten years old in 1970 was virtually certain to have at least one living grandparent. The same child in 1920 had only an 80 per cent chance of having a grandparent. It was almost unheard of then to have four grandparents alive. Today a child's chances of this are 1 out of 14.

Two or three hundred years ago, grandparents were a rarity. Peter Laslett, the British demographer who has dispelled some of the sentimentality about preindustrial life with statistics taken from parish records, has shown that life used to be short and households small. In certain seventeenth-century English communities, very few people reached age seventy. In 1599 in Ealing, then a village near London, no household contained a grandchild. Conversation across the generations must have been much rarer than it is today. "You could not," Laslett has written, "with any confidence expect to see your grandchildren in the world we have lost."

Today you can expect to see your grandchildren and to see them have a third and fourth set of grandparents – their step-grandparents. The jousting for position is fierce. In the step-families where there are three kinds of children – his, hers, and theirs – the grandparent issue can be very prickly. Whose grandparents remember whose birthday? Who collects the biggest haul at Christmas?

Presents are a big issue. Grandparents may be worse than children in weighing the emotional and financial value of each gift, and some of them passionately believe that property should follow blood. I heard of many who are mean enough to give presents only to their own kin within a household of children. A divorced and remarried wife told me with scorn about her step-mother-in-law (her father-in-law's new wife) who was "perfectly dreadful – you know, Southern womanhood." This lady, married only six months, had no great excuse for feelings about her new husband's lineage. But when Christmas came, the stepgrandmother sent two presents only to the household of four young children, one each for her stepson's babies, none for his stepchildren.

In this case, the stepchildren were not defenseless. Fighting on their side were the parents of their own father. These paternal grandparents, hyperattentive since the divorce, took their grand-children away from the home for frequent weekends and summer vacations at their beach house on the Delaware shore. The mother of all the children, caught between these warring sets of grand-parents, doubted whether her two youngest would ever see the big house where their half brother and half sister spent so much of their time.

Grandparents will often try to indulge a grandchild whose parents have split up, leaving the stepparent at a loss about what to do. A stepfather whose divorced wife had a seven-year-old told me: "I never could decide what to give Jimmy for Christmas. But his grandparents – my wife's parents – always seemed to pick the right thing. They knew what little boys loved. I used to think that their presents were too extravagant, that they gave him things he didn't need. They used to call him up from Ohio to see what he wanted. I was irritated with Jimmy. He milked it."

The *Ladies' Home Journal* once referred to the problem in stepfamilies as "that of the grandmothers menace." Mothers who were reluctant to see their sons marry the first time can resent a second wife all the more because for a time they had their boy back. Or they can fall back on the primitive feeling that the child belongs not to his parents but to the clan. A young woman told me of entering a family as stepmother and accepting the infant son of a woman who had been killed in a car crash. She was frustrated and angry at the reaction of her husband's family. "I thought they were lucky to have me," she said, "but they were not grateful at all. They treated me as an intruder." Finally she confronted her mother-in-law. "*When* can I consider the baby my son?" she demanded. The mother-in-law had a ready answer: "It takes nine months to make a baby," she said, "and after nine months you can consider him yours." But the new wife wondered if the mother-in-law would relent even then, for the older woman had strong views about lineage and genes. The stepmother said, "I'm going to fight this blood thing. It just isn't *true*. The people you love are those you feel close to, not those who are related."

Grandparents are the relatives most likely to battle the stepparent for custody if the natural parent dies. But at the same time, many of them are old and tired and worried about their grandchildren. They appreciate the stepparent with energy and courage who is willing to take on the job. "I thought Granny would resent me, because I was taking her daughter's place," said a stepmother who was a substitute for a dead mother. "But she didn't. She was nearly eighty and she had been worried sick about the kids. She was so grateful to me for stepping in and looking after them. She was a real help. When they came home from school, they used to go straight in and see Granny and she made a good buffer, for all of us." "Funny though," she added, "as soon as Granny died, I got pregnant, and I had been trying for two years."

Stepgrandparents, the parents of stepparents, vary greatly in their reactions to the children whom their own children suddenly have in tow. From the reports I heard, they tend to be affectionate, but distant, with their stepgrandchildren. "My mother thinks I've married the wrong person, taken on too much." "My parents like Fred's children, they'll send me a hundred dollars to buy something for them at Christmas, but of course, they just went cuckoo when I had little Sophie. She's the only grandchild they've got and they'll leave everything to her." "It bothered me to see a boy of sixteen lying on his bed all day, listening to music. I felt he should get out in the fresh air. But I couldn't say anything – I'm only a stepgrandmother."

It may happen that the stepgrandparent is the one who sees the grandchildren most and who best enjoys their company. This can be true particularly if their children are among those who are determined to remain childless. Stepgrandchildren are all these older people are going to get. Men and women in this relationship do feel sensitive about its fragility, and they invent funny names to express the pseudokinship. One of the best I heard was "third grandmother." But like stepparents, stepgrandparents can be fickle. They may expect too much too soon, and they may easily retract their offer of love when they are hurt, busy, or presented with grandchildren of their own.

The wheel of remarriage brings children into conjunction with a whole array of new relatives – cousins, aunts, nephews. Suddenly, they are something to each other. But the children may take care not to invest too much. Once hurt, twice shy. To an adult, the children's guardedness can look like greed, taking what they can get, giving nothing back.

My aunts and uncles in Massachusetts scooped my stepchildren into the family eagerly when we brought them over for the summer that my mother was taken ill. They adored them. Handsome, freckle-faced children, fresh from England where they had never tasted Hershey bars or seen a car with automatic windows, never had had a suntan or a pair of colored sneakers, and talking like little movie actors as well! My uncle trotted the pair of them down to a local lunchroom where they soon became mini-celebrities. The girl behind the counter fell in love with my stepson. To my stepdaughter, she would ask: "What kind of ice-cream did you say you wanted, honey?" with a loud aside, "I knew what she said the first time, but I just love to hear that kid talk." The kid *could* talk. Within two days, she could mimic the local accent so well that you could tell it was southeast Massachusetts and not Boston or Providence. "Hot enough fah yah?" she amiably gave as standard greeting to everyone she met. The children were showered with printed T-shirts, games, hoola hoops, watermelons, jumbo bags of every kind of candy, Coca-Cola by the case. My uncle took my stepson with him every day on his milk route. Lessons at the local pool turned both children into swimmers within three weeks.

My family went overboard. Then they climbed back. These kids were hard. I remember one hot summer evening – my husband had not yet arrived from London – when we sat in the family parlor, a circle of relatives and the new stepmother, watching the children fight like cocks in a pit. "I thought English children were supposed to be so well behaved," said one. "Can their father stop them?" asked another. "Usually," I said, helpless.

The kids had been scrapping all day, but what escalated it into a brawl, colossal even by their standards, was the arrival of some old friends of mine who knew I had acquired two stepchildren and had brought two presents. One was a magnificent Indian headdress with bright feathers, designed to enhance the ego of the wearer; the other was a small dull tomahawk whose only discernible function was to kill the owner of the headdress. Which was to have which? "We thought they could share them," the donors said feebly. They could see what was about to happen. The kids ripped at the headdress; they gave each other savage kicks, they crashed into the spectators without even noticing. As I finally managed to lift the heavy younger child and drag her bodily upstairs, I saw through the window the headlights of my friends' car retreating down the driveway.

My aunts and uncles wanted to make the children happy and share America with them. But they were hurt when their gestures didn't work, and disturbed by the naked, un-American, unchildlike passions the children showed. Watching my stepson quiver with rage and anxiety as his sister was given a helping of icecream, my uncle looked at me, shook his head, and said, "Jesus." At the end of that first summer together, both they and the kids were bruised. Something that looked so inviting turned out to be very prickly close up. But the relationship was no mirage. It has proved durable. It is not a bond of family: neither looks for anything of himself in the other. But it means that my stepchildren can always count on a bed and a good meal and perhaps ten dollars when they get to Massachusetts, and both sides enjoy a kind of wonderment in having a tie with people so different.

Territorial disputes

The Romans believed in lares and penates, the gods of the household; so do stepparents and stepchildren. Whose house is it? Whose spirit presides? Whose standard of living dominates?

There is a school of thought that says to the new stepparent, "Move. Make a fresh start, even if you have to take a heavy mortgage, change the children's schools, and commute for four hours a day."

Prior occupation of the territory confers a certain power. Gerda Schulman observed that when two sets of stepchildren are brought together by a new marriage, one set regards itself as the "main family" and the other as the subfamily. The determining factor is whose house becomes the family's home. The childless stepparent is at a disadvantage in the stepchildren's house. Some feel more strongly than others that the ghost of the first spouse lingers within four walls. One woman, reserved, unmarried until thirty-seven, shuddered at the thought of any woman using "another woman's forks and knives," let alone her house. Others do not mind. Insensitive or short of cash, they live in their predecessor's house, even sleep in the same bed. However, even people who move to another city or build a new house find that there is a limit to what paint and wallpaper can do to disguise the fact that there has been a previous marriage. The ghost can invade the new house – how many people throw out all the colored slides of the trip to Europe just because Edna's head can be seen in front of the Petit Trianon? And the division between "theirs" and "ours" and "mine" can be just as strong. I watched one stepmother's face change as she walked from the living-room, with the harpsichord, the green plants, the antiques, and the polished floor, into the kitchen full of hockey sticks, dog dishes flecked with food, school drawings, and odd mittens. Another woman told me that even though she brought with her a son, a daughter, a dog, and a cat, she felt it would remain her husband's house, not hers.

Two households rarely have the same style of living, even if they are backed by the same level of income, and often they are not. One divorced man hated the way his stepchildren, with whom he lived, were supercilious with his own when they came to visit. The stepchildren were rich; his own were not. When his children first came to lunch, he recalled, "my wife's children criticized their table manners. I defended them, and then I got into trouble with my wife!"

A stepparent who has not had children will not have developed standards of organization or housekeeping. Where do you keep odd pieces to jigsaw puzzles that are probably in the house somewhere? The stepchild, on his own terrain, can become like a miniature parent-in-law. "Well," said my stepdaughter, watching me uncertainly add two packages of rice from the shopping to the five already on the shelf, "we certainly don't need any more rice, do we?" And stepchildren do not want their own house changed. "You've painted the walls all white, and we don't like white!" My stepchildren never made the classic accusation: "You're not my real mother!" But until their late teens, they would still whirl upon me furiously and say, "This is not *your* house." After major renovation, it is still a never-ending tug of war for possession of the territory. If they are both at home and my husband is not, I feel that they have reoccupied it. I stay in my room.

The possibility that the stepchild may elect to join the household is something that any prospective stepparent should consider, no matter how unlikely it is at the time of the wedding. Some states allow teen-age children to choose which parent they will live with. New ménages, with new furniture and a cheerful atmosphere, look very inviting to adolescents who have lived in a broken home. It is common for teen-age girls to decide to live with their fathers after a divorce, to escape the hostility with the mother that girls often feel at that age. Thus both father and daughter walk out on the mother together. Men particularly can see the new home as a way to show up the first wife, to show that he is the preferred parent, or to make a new effort to become close to the children he has neglected.

What this means is that there may be secret signals in the air that the stepparent does not pick up. To borrow yet again from Gerda Schulman's perceptive paper: "The relatively frequent occurrence of the collapse of arrangements that have held for long periods of time prior to the new marriage leads this writer to suspect that collusive messages may have been set into motion between the child's father and the child's caretaker (grandparents, foster parents, institutions, or even the child's own mother) at the time of the father's remarriage, culminating in the child's joining the new household. Even if there are no messages on the part of the parents, the child himself is aware of the fact that circumstances have changed and that there is now a possible home for him."

Can the stepparent say no? Few of those I talked to felt they had that choice. A natural parent can kick his child out of the house but a stepparent can't, not easily at least. One woman who did let her dropout stepson come and live with them spoke up when she felt the boy had stayed too long. "I always took the line that this was his home if he wanted it. But then, I felt it was wrong to let him stay here and pay off his debts. So I said to Henry, 'I'm not prepared to let him stay.' Henry didn't agree but he saw my point, and the boy left. He's got a good job now, and a steady girl friend." A sociologist who is not shy of applying theories to her own family life was appalled when her husband wanted to refuse permission for his son to live in their apartment while they were on holiday. Having the boy meant having the hippie scene – the guitars, the girl friends, the homemade granola – but the stepmother was emphatic. "I told him: a father cannot refuse his home to his son."

More and more men are taking custody of their children, and the weekend stepmother should know in her heart what she will say if her husband wants to carry the responsibility all week long. If she says no, she will validate the myth. If she says yes, she may be submitting to emotional blackmail. Or is it moral responsibility?

When a woman chemist married a cardiologist – call them Ann and David – the arrangements for his three children were elaborate but clear. The mother had custody. One weekend a month, David and Ann would take the older two boys, who formed a natural pair. One weekend, they would take the little girl. One weekend they would take all three, and the last weekend – "our honeymoon weekend," Ann said sarcastically – they would have none of the children at all.

About five months after the divorce, the pattern began to change. David, and his ex-wife, too, thought the boys needed their father more than they needed their mother, and the two came to live permanently. It was simple: the two homes were near each other and no change of schools was involved. At the end of the year it became apparent that the mother was losing interest in the little girl. She had a man living in the house; after an early marriage and a heavy dose of motherhood, she was beginning to enjoy her freedom. Abortion law reform, transactional analysis, deep meditation – she went into them all. David told Ann that he was worried about the girl. "Do you think you could cope?" he asked. Coincidentally, the mother chose that time to announce, "I've had enough." So the entire custody agreement was rewritten, and all three children joined their father's new household.

Did Ann feel she had a right to refuse? She did not answer my question. Instead, she said, "We felt that we could not leave them in the lurch. We both have a strong sense of moral responsibility." There are immense satisfactions: the children are blossoming under Ann's care. Where they had trouble in school, they are now getting good grades. They look healthier, act happier. People congratulate Ann at cocktail parties on her ability to cope. One weekend a month now is all that Ann and David have to themselves. Their mother even complains about having to take the children for forty-eight hours. But, Ann says, "I will not give up my weekend," although it is not entirely private. The boys have a paper route, and Sunday mornings they come home and clump through the house, getting their bicycles and turning on the television.

Around the table

Stepparents talk a lot about food and mealtimes; so do Freud and Spock and Melanie Klein. Feeding difficulties are a primary way for a child to express his emotional problems, and adults tend to retain childlike attitudes to their food and how it should be taken.

In many stepfamilies, meals are excruciating, the time when the expectation of happy family life comes up against the reality. If you are living with people you do not like, you will probably find their eating habits irritating, and if someone does not like you, they will not enjoy your cooking. Also, against all evidence, adults cling to a belief in the power of food to make people happy.

If a family is unhappy, chances are that somebody is in the kitchen trying to improve the menu.

Some men become good cooks as their response to divorce. With shish kebab or boeuf bourguignon, they try to convince their children that they still love them, or to bind two sets of children together. One stepmother said, "I dreaded meeting the boys and put it off for a long time. But he, Sid, my husband, is a gourmet cook and he likes to cook a big Sunday lunch and the boys come every week. So one week I was there and that was that."

There is enormous satisfaction in giving children food. Some fathers cannot surrender it to their new wives. But it is the step-mother who usually has the main responsibility for serving the emotionally loaded daily bread. Just as the image of stepmother is witch, so the image of her food is poison. Snow White's step-mother tempts her with a poisoned apple, the queen in *Cymbeline* is "Queen Poisoner" to her stepdaughter, and my little stepdaughter shrieked at me, when she saw me boiling down a turkey carcass: "I'm not going to eat any of that horrible soup full of bones!"

The stepchild who refuses to eat sets a neat psychological trap for his stepmother. Even the part-time stepmother cannot escape. One experienced wife, who tucks her husband's children into her brood when they come up to Maine in the summer, had a stepson who would not eat even the picnic sandwiches. "He accused me of trying to poison him," she said, "and then he said he was going to write to his mother telling her that I starved him."

It is a stepmother's food that will be watched by the outside world. I remember one dinner party in London just after I married when an imperious mother of eight questioned me closely about what I had fed the children for what she called tea. "Meatballs, carrots, and mashed potatoes," I answered. "I do believe that you are overfeeding those children," she trumpeted. "After all, they have their *dinner* at school." This jibe struck home, for my stepdaughter was a butterball. A few days later, I was wondering aloud to an American friend about how to put the girl on a diet. "I don't know about you," she said darkly, "but I could never refuse a child food."

To say that my own stepchildren did not like my cooking would be inaccurate. They liked it, especially the Italian food. But I expected to accomplish too much with tomato paste, and we disagreed violently – still do – on the philosophy of meal-times.

How stepparents complain about the sight of the stepchild at table! Stepfathers seem to mind more. "The boy's table manners annoy me. We have tremendous fights at meals. Oh, he'll leave the table if I say so. I have a very loud voice. The funny thing is that my own children have abominable table manners, too. But they don't bother me the same way." "My eighteen-year-old stepdaughter makes the most marvelous quiche Lorraine. She makes the quiche Lorraine to end all quiches Lorraines. But then she will sit there, refusing to help clear the table. After all, [the stepfather mimics her voice] '*I've* done the cooking.' She is very fat and very greedy. It makes me sick the way she puts away those enormous meals."

But stepmothers suffer too: "Their table manners upset me. I can't bear the way they eat. Partly because they remind me of their mother. She has the worst table manners of anybody I have ever seen. I met her once, years ago, before there was any question of a divorce, and I was revolted and fascinated by this woman who made so much noise eating her food."

A typical stepparent response is to stiffen the ritual. "We all eat at seven-thirty. Even the baby has to stay up. Larry wants us all to be together. He comes in at seven, has a drink, and we all watch Walter Cronkite together. For my son – Larry's stepson – it's mandatory viewing. Then we eat. My children then clear the table, and Larry gives the baby his bath and puts him to bed. But I'm afraid we still have dreadful problems with elbows and napkins." Or, "We're very strict. No bare feet. I'm sorry, but that's the kind of home I want and they have to comply, even though they say 'Mom doesn't make us do this.' " The less the stepparent sees the stepchild, the greater the faith in the cere-mony. "Whenever they came, we made a big thing of dinner. White cloth, candles. Three courses. We treated them like adults and they loved it, even the tiny one."

To say that the stepfamily has to reconstitute itself consciously is only half the truth. The stepfamily has to reconstitute itself at mealtimes. While sex and property may be the cause of stepfamily tensions, the dinner table is where they will be fought out.

CHAPTER 10

Myths and roles

Her mother died when she was young,
Which gave her cause to make great moan;
Her father married the warst woman
That ever lived in Christendom.

The Ballad of Kemp Owyne

The myth of the cruel stepparent and the mistreated stepchild is as alive as ever. As cultural currency, it passes without questioning. Journalists and politicians would be lost without it. "Italy is the stepchild of the European Economic Community." "Common-carrier matters have been the stepchildren at the F.C.C." In an interview describing his hard childhood, the Russian author Alexander Solzhenitsyn said: "My mother raised me in very difficult conditions. She was widowed before I was born and never remarried, mainly because she was afraid a stepfather would be too strict."

Would *any* stepfather have been cruel? Did anybody in fact want to marry Solzhenitsyn's mother? Wouldn't the family have suffered less ("It was cold. Coal was hard to get") if the mother had put aside her fear and allowed a new husband to provide for them? There is no need to ask. Everybody knows about stepfathers. The social implications of the myth are profound. An English magistrate (who presides in local courts) reflected candidly, "Whenever I hear 'stepmother' or 'stepfather' in court, my instant reaction is 'wicked.' I know where it comes from – the Grimm fairy tales. But I recognize it as a prejudice of mine and I have to guard against it." How many judges, one wonders, hold such a bias unaware?

The myth can actively interfere with the building of a new family life. Neighbors and relatives are not at all shy about perpetuating it. A stepmother, according to Helene Deutsch, may be on her way to winning the child's complete love "until the moment when the grown-up members of the family, friends, and above all other children, make the stepchild the executive agent of their own aggressions and stir him to hostility: 'She is not your mother, she cannot love you,' or 'don't take anything from her.' " I was stunned to hear how many stepparents have the myth thrust at them. A nurse who married a man with an eighteen-month-old daughter (his first wife had died of cancer after having the baby) told me that on the Christmas after their wedding, the tiny child had received not one but two copies of *Hansel and Gretel*. "And who was supposed to read it to her? *Me!*" stormed the stepmother.

Often the family makes jokes to ward off the myth. "When I'm in a bad temper," a weekend stepmother said, "Harold teases me. 'All right, stepmother, where's your hat and broomstick?' " A stepdaughter laughingly tells sales ladies: "She's not my mom she's my wicked stepmom." A pediatrician, a stepmother, was powerless to stop the myth. "The child was too charming, too well-behaved in public and difficult at home. I found it hard to hear endless congratulations on how lucky I was to have such a perfect stepdaughter when she was so troublesome. In disciplining her, we had to choose between letting her behave badly or indulging her fantasies about being the mistreated stepchild, the Cinderella. I'm afraid we had to indulge the fantasies. She was sent to her room if she was naughty, and when people came to visit on Sunday afternoon, they would ask, 'Where is Mona?' and we would have to tell them, 'Mona has to stay in her room,' and let them think what they would."

The myth will not go away just because stepmothers recognize its presence. There is too much historical and psychological force behind it. While I did laugh when my stepdaughter's friend compared me to a witch, I did not find it funny at all one evening not long ago when a neighbor settled himself down for a drink and said chattily: "You should hear what old Mrs. So-and-so is saying about *you!*" What on earth, I wondered, since I did not even know the octogenarian he mentioned. "She told me you made your stepson pay for eating a bowl of cornflakes!"

There had indeed been an argument about cornflakes, part of

the endless wrangling about mealtimes, perhaps six or eight years before. What was it, and why was it making the rounds of the suburban village where we live so many years later?

As my husband and I reconstructed it, the argument had gone something like this:

FATHER: "Why cornflakes now?"

BOY: "I'm hungry, that's why."

STEPMOTHER: "But it's ten to six."

BOY: "When are we eating then?"

STEPMOTHER: "Six o'clock."

BOY: "Well, what's for supper?"

STEPMOTHER: "Beef stew."

BOY: "I don't like it." (*Pours milk on cornflakes.*)

FATHER (*getting angry*): "You're not allowed to disregard mealtimes."

BOY: "Why do we have to have mealtimes?"

FATHER: "Because we need to come together as a family and because that is the most economical way to serve nutritious food within the family budget."

BOY: "So what do cornflakes cost then?"

FATHER (*falling into trap*): "Well, about twopence for the cereal and a penny for the milk and, well, forget the sugar."

BOY: "So what if I don't want supper?"

FATHER: "All right, eat those cornflakes, but you're going to have to pay for them."

Did he pay? Oh no, just as he never paid for the broken window and the broken blender, and he never had his sister's china horse fixed as he promised, nor ever mowed the grass. But he did tell the neighbors how he was mistreated, and in the version that went into circulation, it was by his stepmother, not his father. I found out later that he and his sister fed the story to each other. When she was in her late adolescence, berating my husband and me for our inadequacies, up came the cornflakes. "Yes, and I remember the time you made him pay for a bowl of cornflakes! What a thing to do to a boy *in his own house!*"

She could not remember whether or not he had actually paid the sum which was approximately six cents (1966 prices). She said it didn't matter. That's also what the boy said when we asked him, to get the record straight. "I don't think the facts are important," he smiled. "It's the gossip that's interesting." By gossip, he meant the myth, I think, and there I agree with him.

Origin of the tales

Tales of the wicked stepparent seem to flourish among people who practice monogamy. A child must be recognized as the product of a particular pair if the essentials of the drama are to be present: the loss of the loving parent, the arrival of the cold-hearted substitute. In polygamous societies a man's children by his various wives are expected to be treated just as well by one wife as by another. Among the Crow Indians, for example, all the children of a common father call all of his wives Mother. In societies that are strongly patriarchal or matriarchal, children are seen as belonging to one or other side of the family. Thus, in the Arab world, children stay with the father if their mother leaves him and returns to her parents. And in societies where legal marriage is not highly valued and the mother is the center of the family, a motherless child will be raised by grandmothers and aunts.

The stepchild is also protected in those societies which, although monogamous, practice the levirate. This custom, observed by semitic peoples among others, requires the brother of a dead husband to marry the widow if he is not married already. The levirate has obvious drawbacks but it saves a lot of emotional and financial reshuffling. The child's inheritance stays within the family. The wife's family will not have to raise a new dowry to pay for her remarriage. And the child does not get a stranger for a stepfather. In fact, the main function of the levirate, and the complementary custom of the sororate, is to protect the group from a stranger from the outside. (I detected a whiff of the levirate in the after-dinner conversation of a member of Yale's exclusive Skull and Bones Club when he described, with evident satisfaction, how one Bones man had married the widow of another.)

In Western tradition, however, a child owes both his social

standing and his physical and emotional well-being to his biological parents. The loss of one of them is a disaster, a disaster that makes a good story. Wicked stepmother tales go back to classical antiquity. The Greeks had no love of stepmothers. Their mythology includes, among many examples, the legend of Ino, the wife of Athamas, son of Aeolus. Ino, wanting to be rid of her hated stepchildren, Phrixus and Helle, staged an elaborate plot. She persuaded the peasant women to roast the seed corn. When, in consequence, there was no harvest and the starving people sent to the Oracle at Delphi for advice, Ino bribed the messengers to return with the command to sacrifice Phrixus and Helle. The children's real mother, the cloud goddess Nephele, tried to save them by sending a golden-fleeced ram to take them away. But only Phrixus escaped. Helle fell into the sea at the point where the Black Sea meets the Aegean and the name of the strait – Hellespont – is a testimony to the cruelty of stepmothers.

Just as savage a portrait of a stepmother can be found in Eudora Welty's novel, *The Optimist's Daughter*, published in 1972 and Miss Welty is a writer known for her delicacy. The heroine of her book has the pretty name of Laurel; she is a middle-aged childless widow who comes back to the South from Chicago because her adored father, an elderly judge, has to have an eye operation. But what has the judge done in the last years of his life? Married a vulgar, overblown little redhead from Texas, whose very name – Wanda Fay – suggests that she has flown in on a broomstick. The operation fails; the judge is dying. Yet Fay thinks only about herself. She wants to go to the Carnival in New Orleans, she worries about getting her hair done and she itches to get her hands on the lovely old house in Mississippi, with its heirlooms, books and china collected by Laurel's late mother. And she does. Fay hastens the old man's death by jostling him in his hospital bed. Laurel, her stepdaughter, perceptive, sad, wise, sees what is happening:

"I believe he's dying," said Laurel.
Fay spun around, darted out her head, and spat at her.

Although such tales can be found in all times and many

cultures, they seem to have had a particular surge in Europe in the early nineteenth century. I think I have found some historical reasons. One is the beginning of the romantic movement, which made the lives of the ordinary man and woman, and the plight of the child, subjects worthy of literary treatment. Along with romanticism came nationalism and nostalgia for the past. This is what drove the Grimm brothers along. Passionate enthusiasts for ethnic tradition and popular poetry, they collected some two hundred old folk tales, and with their *Kinder-und Hausmärchen*, published in 1812 and 1815, they passed a heavy dose of wicked stepmother myth into the German literary heritage. At the same time, literacy was on the increase. People who were suddenly learning to read wanted good stories. And they wanted to read to children. In northern Europe during the eighteenth century there was a population explosion. Infant mortality declined. The average family in England during the nineteenth century included six or seven children. And if children survived, wives were not so durable. It was an age of children – and of stepmothers.

Cinderella, the world's best loved folk tale, is the archetypal wicked stepmother story. It can be traced back to ninth-century China and has been found, with appropriate local variations, in every corner of the globe from Alaska to South Africa, from Asia to South America and in societies as diverse as the Kaffir, the Celtic, the Scandinavian and the Zuni Indian. By the time it was written down and included by Perrault in his collection of fairy stories in 1697, it had already taken root in Europe. The Perrault version is the "Cinderella" best known in America and Britain. Its opening lines, as pleasingly familiar as a Christmas carol, aim straight for the stepmother:

> There was once a man whose wife died and left him to bring up their only child, a little daughter, who was sweet and gentle by nature and as pretty as a girl could be.
>
> Father and daughter lived happily enough together until the man married again. His new wife was a proud and masterful woman, with two plain daughters who were as arrogant and disagreeable as she was herself.

In 1892 an earnest British folklorist, Marian Roalfe Cox, catalogued 345 variations of the Cinderella story. Working without benefit of Freud, whose *Interpretation of Dreams* was not published until 1911, Miss Cox could only marvel at the common ingredients in the tales. Most, she observed, cast the heroine as a stepdaughter, who was given old clothes, humiliating work to perform, and a degrading name as well. Cinderella seems to be the nicest of them. There are, to name a few, Askenbasken (louse of the ashes), Fedte-Matte (greasy Matty), Fjos-Labba (stable slut). Although details of the story vary wildly, the basic plot tends to be the same. The girl, with supernatural help in the form of a fairy godmother, a friendly animal, or a magical plant, exchanges her rags for finery and goes off to a ball, fair, or church ceremony where a young nobleman falls in love with her. She flees from him, not once but three times. The third time she drops an identifying object, usually a slipper, but sometimes a ring or a strand of hair. By means of the clue, the nobleman finds her. The story ends with the disguise revealed and the girl's happy marriage.

Symbols like these made ripe pickings for the early psychoanalysts. Otto Rank, with *The Myth of the Birth of the Hero*, and Frank Ricklin, with *Wish Fulfillment and Symbolism in Fairy Tales*, left little for anybody else to add in the way of interpretation. Ricklin scorns the attempts of folklorists to trace the stories back to "one hazy Aryan myth." Instead he says "fairy tales are inventions of the directly utilized, immediately conceived experiences of the primitive human soul." They have much in common with dreams, he asserted, and they have the same use – they help the child (or adult) to live with his sadistic and incestuous impulses. Rank points out the splitting of the parent into good and bad that is a rampant theme in myth and folklore. These myths, he said, have "a paranoid structure" – separating what is joined in life, the love and hate for the parents.

By their lights, Cinderella is a story with a key. The key is the girl's rivalry with her mother, and mixed desire for, and fear of rape by, her father. In Cinderella, there are two mother figures Good- (the fairy godmother) and Bad (the stepmother). The longing for the father is turned into the acceptable, non-incestuous guise of a young prince. The wand is a phallus, the feared rape by the father becomes the prince's pursuit of the girl, which ends in a happy marriage. Throughout, the story holds symbols galore of castration, loss of virginity and the onset of menstruation.

"Snow White and the Seven Dwarfs" presents the rivalry with the mother even more starkly. The loving mother who wanted the baby dies soon after she is born. In comes the step-mother. It is a battle of estrogen, and Snow White is the inevitable winner, for she is younger. The Queen's mirror tells the truth. But the older woman has more power, including the older woman's power of sexual intercourse to charm the father, for he never appears. (Fathers are conspicuously absent or passive in wicked stepmother stories.) Having failed to murder Snow White (the huntsman cannot bring himself to stab her) the wicked Queen tricks Snow White with a symbol of the breast (Rank's idea), an apple that contains poison, not nutrition.

An even neater example of splitting is "Hansel and Gretel." This story contains not one but two Bad Mothers. Good Mother is dead. The stepmother, seeing the lack of food and wanting enough to eat for herself, persuades the father to abandon his children in the wood. "The poor woodcutter, with a heavy heart, for he loved his children, consented." (Why? The stepmother's sexual spell over the father again.) Then, lost in the wood, the hungry children are tempted by an even more wicked Bad Mother – an outright witch, with an edible house. When, starving, they try to eat it, she captures them, to eat them herself.

In her "Cinderella – 345 Variants," Miss Cox picked out a fascinating thread without knowing where it led. She noticed in what she called the Catskin version of the tale that there was no wicked stepmother – but no mother either. Only the father, without a wife. The father, the king, will marry no woman who is not as lovely as his departed wife and there is only one female who fills the bill: his daughter. There are any number of such tales which are blatant incest fantasies, variously called "Ass's Skin," "Cat's Skin" or "Donkey-Skin." (Ricklin says that having fairy tales told by women to children is a device for masking these common sexual fantasies.) In all of them, the girl has to mar her beauty to discourage the old man. Sometimes she disguises herself with an animal's skin, sometimes she covers herself with dirt or scratches herself. The story has the conventional Cinderella ending. A prince catches a glimpse of her without her ugly disguise, falls in love, cannot find her again, pursues her by means of a clue – it's a ring in Perrault's "Donkey-Skin" – and finally marries her. The king her father turns up as a guest at the wedding and asks her forgiveness. The story does not say what the king will do for a new wife.

For the girl does not care. What stands out in these stories, according to a number of psychoanalytic interpretations, is the utter self-centredness of the girl. She is, so to speak, snow-white, gentle and kind, all her murderous and incestuous wishes projected onto those around her. One academic paper was unkind enough to describe Cinderella as a sexual tease. She tempts the prince-father with her beauty, then runs away and hides, making him suffer to find her.

But why *stepmothers*? Why is the myth so much harder on women than men? There are plenty of wicked stepfathers in real life. They are there in literature – the King in *Hamlet*, Mr. Murdstone in *David Copperfield*. ("David," he said, making his lips thin by pressing them together, "if I have an obstinate horse or dog to deal with, what do you think I do? . . . I beat him. . . . I make him wince and smart.") They're there in mythology – King Polydectes, in love with Perseus's mother, Danaë, sent Perseus to fetch the head of the Gorgon Medusa – and in autobiography. It is easy to conclude, after reading what James Baldwin has to say about his stepfather, a righteous minister who thrashed him and taunted him for being ugly, that Baldwin's sense of isolation comes more from being a stepson than from being black. Where is the wicked stepfather in children's stories?

He is there – but not as a stepfather. The hated male parent – Bad Father – appears as an ogre or a giant; the Good Father as a helpful animal or a king who has lost his son. The boy's "Cinderella" is "Puss in Boots" or "Jack and the Beanstalk." In "Puss," the Good Father is a very clever cat, far cleverer than the simple youth he is aiding. The real father, the poor miller, is dead. The boy who needs help is the youngest son, who has been left, as his inheritance, nothing but the cat. The talking cat helps his master to disguise himself as a nobleman (like Cinderella going to the ball) and then plays a trick on the Bad Father – the Ogre. The cat taunts the Ogre into turning himself into a mouse – which the cat gobbles up. As a result, the youngest son takes over the Ogre's castle and marries the king's daughter.

The frank incestuous theme of Jack and his beanstalk is too comical to spell out. Suffice it to say that Jack's widowed mother is not looking for a new husband. But she fears (wrongly) that Jack is too immature for her, for she does not appreciate the superfertility of the beans which an old man (Good Dead Father) has given Jack in exchange for the cow. She throws the beans away but they grow into a phallic symbol such as the world has never seen. Jack climbs. In a giant (adult) sized world high in the sky, he is protected by a giantess who lets him hide in her enormous oven and who has a mysterious loyalty to the strange boy instead of to the Ogre, her husband. Jack tricks the Ogre, who is a cannibal, and escapes home with the Ogre's store of wealth – a hen that lays golden eggs, which supports the ménage of Jack and his mother happily ever after. Oh yes. Jack kills the Ogre by chopping down the beanstalk.

To Otto Rank, the male counterpart of the mistreated stepdaughter is the Hero – the self-made young man who has dispensed with parents altogether. If the stepdaughter's triumph is to marry well, for the young hero, it is to be born at all. Rank lists a noble company of heroes – Moses, Jesus, Oedipus, Siegfried – who have a similar background: descent from noble parents, early death plotted by wicked people, exposure to the elements (in a box or a river or a manger), the raising by lowly parents and the restoration, in the end, with their rightful royal position. All of these myths, Rank says, spring out of the child's longing for the "vanished happy time when his father still appeared to be the strongest and greatest man and his mother seemed the dearest and most beautiful woman" and his need at the same time to become independent of his parents.

Rank has a solid answer to the question: why step*mothers*? The facts of reproduction, he says, make maternity sure, paternity uncertain. "The child, when it is aware of sexual relations, can alter the 'family romance' by ennobling the father." The older child can strengthen this fantasy that his father is not his real father by imagining that in reality his mother had a secret lover – a version of the child himself. But he cannot pretend that he had a different mother – "the child accepts the descent from the mother as an unalterable fact."

Hate for the mother can be considerable, even greater than that for the father. Women have so much more influence over the life of the child, they may be in contact with him twelve or more hours a day. They must constantly frustrate the wishes of the child. In times past, moreover, the household was an economic unit of which the mother was the foreman. The child had to perform many disagreeable tasks – delivering bread, combing wool, sorting potatoes – and there was no trade union to speak for his interests. But then, as now, hate for the mother was blasphemous – while it was and is acceptable, even admired, to hate a father. To cope with the hate for the mother, therefore, children have only one escape route: to dream that their good mother is gone and replaced by another kind of mother – a stepmother.

Quite apart from the needs of the unconscious, there was in the past good economic justification for hating stepmothers more than stepfathers. When the household was an economic unit, the mother was the foreman who assigned work to children. A stepmother had considerable opportunity to be cruel. A real mother who remarried and remained in charge of the kitchen, however, could protect her own children from her new husband.

There were also the harsh practices of primogeniture. When a father took a new wife, his existing children saw their inheritance threatened. At very least, he had to support her. In thirteenth-century England, in certain communities, an heir got no part of his father's estate until the father's widow died, even if she was just a stepmother. And wherever inheritance passed only to males, girls had particular reason to fear a stepmother if their father had no sons. He would almost certainly try to produce the longed-for male heir with his new wife, while his daughters would depend on the stepmother to issue them food and clothing, knowing that she would try to preserve as much of the wealth as possible for her own offspring.

The concept of the wicked stepfather is deeply rooted in fact, none the less. This kind of story (taken from *Time*) causes no surprise:

> For £30,000 in municipal bonds, he bought twelve-year-old Rita ("Jackie Lee" Flynn of Bolinbrook, Ill.) from her mother and step-father, Rita and Fred Flynn. The happy trader and his 5-ft., 100-lb. blonde bride-to-be then headed for South Carolina, where girls can marry at 14. They planned to await Jackie Lee's equally content stepfather, who intended to fly in and sign consent papers stating that she was 14.

A stepfather may sell a stepchild, take his money (Jackie Coogan, one of Hollywood's early child stars, lost the fortune he had earned to his mother and stepfather in spite of winning a celebrated lawsuit). He may rape the child, and commonest of all fears, he may beat the child.

Stepfathers are prominent in statistics of child abuse. In *Violence Against Children* Dr. David Gil of Brandeis University presented data that showed fathers had a higher rate of child-battering than mothers did, and stepfathers even a higher rate than fathers. Of children beaten by a "father or father substitute," one-third suffered at the hands of stepfathers.

The disproportion of stepfathers in child-battering also showed up in a British investigation into the deaths of twenty-nine young children killed by a "father or father substitute." It was the substitute who was the murderer in more than half the cases. "These figures confirm," wrote Dr. P. D. Scott of the Maudsley Hospital, "that for unstable fathers to care for their children, especially if they are not the biological parent, may be hazardous."

In Britain the most notorious child-battering in recent years, the Maria Colwell case, involved a stepfather. The public inquiry into the child's death concentrated on the rigidity of the social workers and the law that placed the rights of a parent higher than the welfare of the child. Only Maria's mother, a dull woman in her tenth pregnancy when her husband was sentenced for man-slaughter, seemed to understand the feelings of inadequacy that can drive a stepfather over the brink. Her husband had been out of work and thought he was the victim of anti-Irish prejudice. Then: "During 1972 Maria started to get thinner and also to tell lies. She became dirty in her habits and would forget to use paper when she went to the toilet. I think all this was starting to get Mr. Kepple down. He was a man who got annoyed quite easily about small things, and although I never thought then that he would ever hurt Maria, I could see his annoyance building up as she went on ignoring him and behaving as she did."

The cruel stepparent myth survives because there is truth in it. Yet the well-meaning stepparent has only natural parenthood to use as a model for the alternative to the myth and that does not suit either.

The search for roles

Because fatherhood implies potency and authority, it is easy for today's stepfathers by divorce to feel unmanned. "Sometimes by mistake my stepdaughter calls me Mother." "I see myself as an extension of their mother, not their father." Some of these men define their roles in neuter terms. "In the family, I'm just a third wheel." Or they acknowledge weak efforts to lay down the law: "I told him it was very unwise to smoke pot, and besides, it was against the rules of the house."

Stepfathering with the natural father present in the background is a new pattern brought about by the rise in divorce. Stepfathers by death have been common enough figures through history. Just as stepmothers were essential to help a widower look after his children, stepfathers were indispensable to help a widow carry on a business or a farm. Whether there were more stepparents of one sex or the other is hard to say. They were probably fairly evenly balanced. Women tended to die early because of child-bearing and its associated ills, and historical records suggest that men remarried quickly, that in fact they remarried until they dropped. But they dropped early too. A woman who survived to middle age was then likely to outlive her husband, and a child's chances of losing a father before the age of eighteen have always been high. A widow with property, especially a young widow, was a good candidate for remarriage and many children accordingly had stepfathers.

But today the stepfather is gaining in numbers over the step-mother, at least as the stepparent with the stepchild as a permanent resident. The U.S. Census figures showed that in 1970 there were twice as many children living with a divorced parent as there had been in 1960. Most of these parents can be assumed to be mothers, as women retain the children in 90 per cent of divorce decrees. And as most of these divorcees either were remarried or are likely to be, the ranks of stepfathers by divorce must have increased substantially as well.

But more men remarry

Extremes are hard to avoid. I witnessed two ways of playing the part. Both men, bachelors, married women with sons from a first marriage. Both now have children of their own and look happy. But their contrasting approaches to their stepsons seem, each in its own way, to be artificial and self-conscious. Perhaps these are the only alternatives that today's society allows.

One is the St. Joseph type. He defers to his wife:

> My general rule was not to become too deeply involved. I leave all the discipline to Marian. After all, he's *her* son. Anyway, Andrew has a perfectly good, well, I can't say "perfectly good," but good enough, well, let's just say that he has his *real* father living practically across the street. Even though Marian's marriage was breaking up when the boy was born and we were married before he was eighteen months old, I've never thought of him as my son. He's never called me anything but Joe. He calls his own father Dad. And I've tried hard not to inflict my ideas on him. A father, as I see it, theoretically is the one who takes a strong line. It was more natural for his father to try to act the father.

(Hear it again? Fatherhood is acting. Motherhood is real.)

The other stepfather, Leonard, played the part with deliberate severity, not only because he had an aggressive temperament, but because the boy's true father had vanished. For Leonard, every reminder that he was a mere stepfather made him angry. He bitterly resented the boy's unwillingness to call him Dad.

"I had the responsibility and I wanted what went with it," he said. "I was pressing for total adoption, but it was out of the question. The boy's father's family would not hear of it. He was their only grandson . . ." ("He was an adorable kind of child," interrupted the boy's mother, who was listening in.) " . . . he carried their name for posterity and they contributed to his support. I wanted to do all the support myself, to erase completely the bond between the boy and his father. But it was impossible."

Leonard, a nice guy with a can of beer, presented himself as a tough disciplinarian. "Baby-sitting. When our own children were born, he was supposed to baby-sit for us. We made him stay in from parties and places he might have gone. If he had a job or a paper route, I made him stick to it. He had to earn all his spending money. His friends got allowances. Hit him? Sure I hit him."

His wife made a face. "I thought you were mean," she said.

Leonard looked startled. "Was I mean *all* the time?"

"No, not all the time. You were pretty strict with our own too." In a mild voice, she explained: "I felt that if anybody was going to hit my son, I had the sole right to do it. But Lenny brought love and stability to our lives and I was glad to have a man around."

Leonard says he loves his stepson. He was moved to tears the day he drove the boy to college and said good-bye. Stepfathering, he found, was easier once he had a son of his own: "That dealt with one tension. At last I had a role that was no longer ambiguous."

Much depends on whether the wife can share control of the child. Some women allow their new husband to discipline only their mutual children, while reserving authority over the one that they brought into the marriage.

Arrangements for the financial support of the stepchild can also affect the stepfather's view of his role. In some circumstances, he can oust the father completely. A hairdresser told me that when her second husband proposed, he ordered her to draw up a budget for a family with two children, totally excluding the payments made by her first husband because he didn't want to be dependent on them. Many stepfathers, on the other hand, could not pay the full costs of the stepchildren and would not be allowed to if they were able.

The man who pays nothing toward a child's expenses may hesitate to accompany his wife to parent-teachers' meetings or to give an opinion on dropping physics or changing schools. "My wife would like me to participate more," a childless stepfather said, "but I don't feel I have any right. *He* pays the bills, *he* makes the decisions." In fact, "even when we go out to dinner and I pay for Claire, my wife kind of murmurs that I needn't. But I love giving Claire money. I practically force it on her. I wish her allowance came from me but her mother gives it to her."

It may be that love comes more readily to stepfathers than to stepmothers. A man who can accept another man's child because he loves the child's mother may find great happiness from the relationship. Many stepfathers, unlike stepmothers, told me how much they loved their stepchildren. "It was far, far easier than being a parent – all of the satisfactions and none of the guilt." "I love some of my wife's children; my wife feels guilty because she doesn't love mine." "She's a lovely little girl – I keep young through her." One of the most contented stepfathers I met boasts about his wife's sons as if they were his own. He had none of his own. His wife was one of those whose second marriage produced only miscarriage after miscarriage. "My proudest moment as a stepfather," he likes to say, "was when Tom came to me and said, 'Arthur, tell me how you get rid of a girl who is fonder of you than you are of her?' It was a real male-to-male confidence. I was so pleased to think that he came to me instead of going to his mother. And I wonder how many sons ask their real fathers for advice on their love life?"

Along with love goes gratitude. Maybe a man, more easily than a woman, can find satisfaction in vicarious parenthood and in a detached way employ the perspective the stepchild gives him on a younger generation. One stepfather, who enjoys the eccentricity of his role, imagines how he will one day thank his stepdaughter. "I think to myself that when Hilary is maybe five years older and has left home that she'll come up to me and say, 'Thank you, John, for all you've done for me. I know you didn't need to do it, for you're only my stepfather . . . ' And I'll say to her (this is my fantasy) 'But you gave me far more than I gave you.'"

Just as today's stepfathers suffer from the vagueness of father-hood, stepmothers suffer from the explicitness of motherhood. A mother will always take you in. A face only a mother could love. A psychiatrist expressed no surprise that his wife could not love his children from his first marriage. "It is harder for a woman to be a stepparent. She can never lose the feeling that she's not had this child in her body." Another said that preg-nancy was a "maturational crisis for a woman. There will always be a special bond between the mother and the child she has borne herself."

Because women hardly welcome the suggestion that their emotions are governed by their reproductive organs, the step-mothers who felt it might be true were apologetic. "I try to love them, but there's no comparison. I knew it when my baby was born. It was like an atom bomb going off. Boom. Love. There it was. Sure, I shout at him, too, but then he comes and hugs me and says, 'I love you, Mommy,' and I melt."

Is it the womb that makes the difference or the work? Courts usually hold that the husband has a duty to support the wife and that she has an obligation to provide household services. Even if paid help is available, children mean work – woman's work, shopping, entertaining, comforting. Most stepmothers shoulder the extra chores because of economics: "I get very depressed. I do three loads of washing every day. Sometimes I think, why didn't Richard stay home and take care of them and I could have just kept on teaching. After all, they're *his* children. But my salary wouldn't support all of us."

The modern phenomenon, of course, is the weekend step-mother and theoretically she should get a smaller and less disturbing dose of stepparenthood than the full-time stepmother. Many women enjoy the role. Like Norman Mailer, they find it fun to be a temporary matriarch, presiding over a large and busy household. In actual practice, however, the weekend step-mother can be a very unhappy and overworked lady. First of all, she has to stifle her bitterness about the alimony and payment for child support. The average divorced man has to pay between one-third and one-half of his salary after tax to his former wife. Then, just when the stepmother wants to relax from her job or has her own children home from school, in come stepchildren. They want to cook, they want six beds made up, they want to spend time with Daddy. An article in *Cosmopolitan* maintained that the United States is full of unhappy weekend stepmothers, fed up with the sullen trips to the zoo, with the sexy thirteen-year-old girl who crawls into bed with Daddy "because she is afraid of the dark" and with the husband or lover who spends money he doesn't have in trying to win back his children's affection when they come to visit. The women who were interviewed complained about the frequency of the visits. "The boys, obnoxious little horrors, visit *every* weekend, *every* holiday . . ." And about the waste of money and the children's ingratitude. "We spend every damn weekend taking his darlings places – movies, puppet shows, Chinatown, Sausalito, yet they never have a good time."

"Weekend" suggests something brief and fleeting. "Part-time" is a more appropriate adjective for the stepmother by divorce. Most I talked with entertained their stepchildren for extended visits during the year, sometimes for as long as two months, and these visits are supposed to be happy, every minute. Even on a mere weekend, the maternal duties are not negligible. One man tried to figure out why his present wife had so much more difficulty with his children than he had with hers. He was proud that she had her own career as a lawyer. "But let's face it," he said, "my kids did arrive every Friday night and we took them off to our place in the Berkshires. The food, the luggage, the blankets, organizing all that fell to Miriam. You know that old Helen Hokinson cartoon where the woman is packing the car when her husband comes home and she announces 'I can go to the country for the weekend or I can get ready to go to the country for the weekend but I can't do both?' Well, that's how Miriam felt."

In a sense, there is no such thing as a part-time stepmother. Whatever the world demands of mothers, stepmothers are supposed to provide whenever the child comes their way. For example, a supposedly child-free second wife told me how she was expected every year to "give them Christmas." "Their mother couldn't be bothered and my husband liked them to come to us. I did it, year after year, even though they are in their late teens. Last Christmas something snapped. I had been sick, my back was in a brace, and I did the whole show – the presents, the decorations, the turkey. They came. They took it all – and they left the house without so much as saying they had enjoyed it. I broke down into floods of tears. I told my husband, 'Even *stepmothers* have feelings!' " She might have said even part-time stepmothers have to play Mother.

Apart from the part-time stepmother, there are two species of stepmother which deserve more notice than they get. One is the unmarried stepmother. She really does not know what she is getting into, for she accepts to live with a man whose children are "with their mother." But they come to visit, all the same. When they come, they have less reason than legitimate stepchildren (if that is the phrase) to defer to the woman of the house for they think of it solely as their father's home. Again, it is the rare tactician among women who can – if she wants to – get away without performing maternal duties for her man's children. I have seen a love nest to which the husband's daughter, an aggressive teenager with pendulous bosom, also has a key. Sometimes in the evening the father's girl friend cooks for the three of them. Sometimes, for a treat, the father says gaily "Let's all go out to dinner!" And on vacations he scoops up his three smaller children from their mother and they go, all six, on a sailing holiday. This can evolve into the situation – almost everybody knows of one – in which the father is happily living with a girl friend, when the mother, out of the blue, dies, runs away or has a nervous breakdown. Suddenly, the child or children are shifted to their father. A girl friend who is hoping to be made a wife will dredge up maternal qualities she may have had no intention of ever using.

The other underprivileged stepmother was employed as housekeeper or nursemaid before the marriage. The common assumption will be that the man chose her solely because she was there and that she is his social inferior. "He married the girl who was looking after the children" is about as unflattering a description as any second wife has to bear, even though she belongs to an honorable tradition of plain, industrious girls, like Jane Eyre, who married the master. Psychologically, the housekeeper-turned-wife has special problems. If the new home is not happy, she will seem to be at fault, for the husband's life goes on as before. Also, in the children's eyes, she will have changed from a maternal to a sexual figure. Deutsch says that one of the step-mother's main problems is to get the children to assent to her sexual relationship to their father. If she has seemed to belong to them before the marriage, they will feel betrayed when she goes over to their father's side. Henry James is good on this in *What Maisie Knew*. The governess changes before the child's eyes from a tender protective nursemaid to a coy, seductive second wife, who overnight loses interest in Maisie.

On the other hand, if the housekeeper has not managed to snag the head of the household for herself when he was wifeless, the new wife can expect trouble. Remember Mrs. Danvers keeping alive the ghost of the first Mrs. DeWinter in *Rebecca*? Here are fresh versions: "The cleaning woman never ceases to tell me how Theresa wanted to bring up that child." Or "The nanny left the day before I arrived. She wouldn't even let the girls come to the wedding." "Once the live-in girl had gotten over her fantasy that my husband had really meant to marry her, she was a great help to me."

For stepmothers, just as for stepfathers, the adolescent child of the same sex presents the greatest problems in the ordinary give-and-take of family life. Stepmothers and stepdaughters have a tough time. They are acutely aware of each tiny detail of each other's physical appearance and compete madly. Sometimes the relationship relaxes into sisterly confidences and exchanges of clothes. More often it is tense. After babbling on about her three stepsons, one woman clammed up about her stepdaughter. "I told my husband before you came that I wasn't going to mention it . . . But she *will* wear these mini-skirts and she's got these fat legs and . . . " No further comment. A stepmother is in for trouble if her own self-esteem is low. She needs a sense of humor and it does not hurt to be good-looking as well, like the woman who laughed to tell me: "I changed my hair color but it went wrong, a deep tangerine. You can see the remnants of it now. Just before we went on vacation, I was in my bedroom and my stepdaughter was here with a girl friend. I heard the friend ask – I don't think they thought I could hear – what *has* she done to her hair?" And then I got this whiff of how I seemed to them – a being from another planet – somebody utterly strange."

For what it is worth, not one stepmother complained to me about not being called Mother. Perhaps their sense of true motherhood is too sharp or because women do not stand on titles. I was interested to see a bitter comment by a stepmother in *The Ladies' Home Journal*: "First I had to get used to four strangers calling me 'Mama' – although for a long time they also called me 'she.' Neither 'Mama' nor 'she' meant 'me' to me, and I felt frightened by the loss of my identity."

As a breed, stepmothers are not masochists. They put up with stepchildren and the work for several identifiable reasons. Primarily because they love their husband but also because they do not have a bad deal. Second husbands are, to many women, synonymous with security. They are men who have been through, or believe they have been through, hell. They are struggling to support two households. They are unlikely to bolt again. There's another reason too. It has to do with a sense of dignity as a woman. Many stepmothers – particularly the childless ones – feel that they have something to *give* the stepchildren. They do not talk about maternal instinct for that is unfashionable but they reveal a firm conviction that mothering is something a woman is good at.

Some are almost arrogant in claiming to be a more sensitive parent than their husband is: "All the presents come from me. *I'm* the one who remembers." "I do the visiting for him. Some weekends come and Malcolm says – he's a moody guy – 'I do love them but I just don't feel like seeing them' and so I go." An academic from Berkeley who looks as if she equated children with pollution told me that it was she who got up in the night if one of her husband's children needed anything when they were visiting (and they *did* wake up – one of them was only three at the time of the divorce). "*He* wouldn't do it. He wouldn't hear them and besides, he's the kind of man who is frightened if anyone is sick and he would be absolutely useless." Another childless professional woman with a high rank in government service told me that her husband could be too strict with his children. One night when the children were horsing around, he swore that if the little girl let down the air mattress one more time, she would have to sleep all night on the bare floor. Of course the child let the air out of the mattress again. "But I persuaded him to relent. I said 'She's only *six*.'"

Blessed Mother. Intercede for us. It is a familiar role for women.

Because mothering, like sexiness, is still a challenge many women have to meet, part-time stepmothers often want to show themselves superior to the real mother. When the children come, they put aside the Russian biographies they are translating, give up going to the hairdresser's, make mountains of sandwiches and spend the day behind the wheel. So many say: "We really knocked ourselves out when they came, to compensate them for the dreary life they had with their own mother." And what part-time stepmothers most of all criticize in a first wife is lack of motherliness. "I bought all their clothes and had their hair cut. She never cared how they looked." "She never knew how to say goodbye when she brought them back on Sunday night – quickly, so it wouldn't hurt. She'd drag it out."

When stepmothers do gain stepchildren's confidence, the rewards are tremendous. "The little girl, when she came back for the summer, walked straight into the bedroom and threw her arms around me." To help a child grow and become happier is one of the most deeply satisfying things anyone can do. When there is enough money, when the work is shared, the children are polite and the stepmother flexible, when the husband can balance his love for his wife for love for his children and does not plunge into a frenzy of fathering out of guilt, then stepmothers pour out sincerely the words that everyone wishes they could say all the time: "They are such marvellous kids, I love having them." "They have enriched my life." "It makes me so happy to know that they all are there and we are such friends and always will be."

There is no point in being pollyannaish. This state of mutual love is not often reached and the biggest catch in stepmother love is that the relationship was created by a marriage, not by a biological event. What happens when the marriage ends? Broken hearts, for some. "I loved those children so much I cannot

tell you. And now that their father has left me I love them still."
Guilt, for others. A divorcee who had had full charge of her
husband's two daughters told me how much she had loved them.
"They filled my life. They *were* my life." But she did not give
them any warning when she left their father for another man. "I
simply went to Florida and didn't come back. No, I didn't tell
them. I felt *he* should do it. After all, *he* was their *father*. Besides,
my lawyer advised me against it."

For stepmothers who stay the course there is one recompense
not generally recognized: the gratitude of their husbands. While
stepfathers told me of being scolded by their wives, stepmothers
mentioned over and over again how their husbands reassured
them they were doing well with the children. (Maybe this is
another sign of the patronizing male, thankful to have found a
woman to do what he wouldn't do himself.) Suspect or not, this
gratitude keeps many stepmothers going. "My stepchildren get
angry with Leo for being partial to me," said a woman who had
taken two stepchildren into her home, "but he feels total in-
debtedness to me for having them." Another who castigated
herself for bad temper said, "When I go on like that, Peter says
to me, 'Just think what their lives would be like if you weren't
there.'"

CHAPTER 11

Rights and duties of stepparents

> At this point, I have a curious confession to make. You will laugh – but really and truly I somehow never managed to find out quite exactly what the legal situation was.
>
> Humbert Humbert in *Lolita*

Stepparents have good reason to be bewildered about their status in law. If they have a vague feeling that they may somehow have obligations without rights, they may not be far wrong. The law as it affects the stepparent is confusing and contradictory, almost always to the stepparent's disadvantage, as society concerns itself with protecting the rights of the natural parent on the one hand and itself from unnecessary expense on the other.

On the face of it, there is no resemblance in law between the stepparent and the natural parent. The status of stepparent is not formally acknowledged by either American or English law. There is no statute that says that a legal relationship comes into existence between stepparent and stepchild at the time of the marriage of the stepparent and one of the child's natural parents.

The stepparent, it follows, has none of the rights of a parent. Correspondingly, the stepchild has no rights of inheritance from the stepparent in the United States or in England, with the insignificant exception that some states allow an estate to go to a stepchild if there is no other distant relative and the alternative would be that the estate pass into public funds.

It may seem irrelevant to mention rights, for talk of "parental rights" is going out of fashion. In cases involving children, particularly in custody disputes, courts are increasingly concerned with putting the rights of a parent secondary to the child's welfare. But the two principles conflict in a way that courts must resolve in each individual case. (One way out of the conflict is for a judge to decide that a child's interest is best served by living with a natural parent.)

Parental rights are very real and stepparents should acquaint themselves with them. The most important right held by both parents of a legitimate child is custody – the physical possession and care of the child. If there is a divorce, the father will usually surrender the physical presence of the child, but retain rights to visit the child, to consent or refuse permission for major surgery or for marriage below the legal age, as well as to determine the child's religion and to be notified of any legal action concerning the child.

A stepparent has none of these. When they become a matter of crucial importance is when the stepparent's spouse dies (as in *Lolita*). Has a stepparent who has looked after a child for a number of years acquired any parental right to keep the child?

The simple answer is no. There are fairly frequent court cases in which a stepparent tussles with a natural parent over custody, and it is clear that parental rights are attached only to natural parents and can be acquired by others only by some form of legal process. This does not mean that invariably a stepparent has to give up the child and the child go to live with a natural parent whom he hardly knows. The courts often decide in favor of leaving the child with the stepparent. There was a case in Colorado in 1963, for example, in which a stepfather won custody because the stepchild had been in the family for five years. In contrast, in Minnesota in 1959, the courts allowed a father to reclaim his children when they had lived for nine years with their mother and stepfather. But where stepparents win – against a natural parent, a grandmother, or an aunt – it is not on the grounds that the stepparent has any parental right: only on the basis of the welfare of the child.

Courts may terminate parental rights in certain circumstances: when a child has been neglected or has lost contact with a natural parent, or simply, in some states, when the divorced parent who has custody wishes it. What is important to remember is that a stepparent is in a weak position in a custody fight and that parental rights do not grow out of acting like a parent.

In the matter of financial support, stepparents in general can be assured that they have no obligations in common law toward their stepchildren. Their freedom from such responsibility rests on the fact that the marriage of the stepparent to the parent creates no legal relationship between the stepparent and stepchild.

Yet stepfathers, in particular, cannot always avoid the burden of paying the stepchildren's bills, especially if the natural father is dead or unwilling to support them. Two states – New York and California – have enacted statutes imposing a duty of support on stepfathers if the alternative is that the child go on relief. Other states place no statutory duty, but in some cases courts have held that the stepparent has voluntarily assumed the obligation by taking the child into his home and letting himself be known as the person caring for and educating the child. In legal terms, this is known in the United States as accepting the *in loco parentis* relationship, in England as giving the child the status of a "child of the family." It is a role that can be assumed by anyone – a relative or stranger – who gives a child the protection normally expected of a parent. In America, however, the stepparent who wants to shed the role can usually do so at will. He simply ceases to maintain the child; however, he would not be able to be reimbursed for the maintenance already provided. In England, to the contrary, a stepfather who assumes support will be required by the courts to continue providing it even if the marriage ends, unless there is someone else willing to support the child.

The strict letter of the law on stepparent obligations does not tell the whole story. There is another common, although indirect, way of forcing stepparents to support their stepchildren – by taking away a mother's welfare benefits when she remarries. The old puritanical prejudice endures: why shouldn't a man who wants to sleep with a woman pay her bills? Aid to dependent children is quite commonly denied to women who have a new husband or even a lover in residence. In Britain welfare authorities can be ruthless, stopping payments without warning when they suspect that a man is not merely visiting but actually staying the night. The whole practice is as unrealistic as it is unsavory. It deters remarriage, which, by stabilizing a troubled home, can actually perform a service for the state. Moreover, it punishes one man quite unfairly for another man's irresponsibility.

Because of the inconsistencies in law and custom, stepparents should examine their legal positions carefully. Well-off men who find themselves slipping into the position of de facto support of their stepchildren should consider what they will do if the marriage ends. So should stepmothers who find themselves acting more and more like real mothers. Would they have rights to visit their former stepchildren after a divorce? Most people do not worry about such intricacies until it is too late. They might find themselves in the predicament of the woman lecturer from North Carolina who wrote to me: "Personally, I have a ten-year marriage to a man whose two sons I brought up along with my own three children. My stepsons professed love for me, rarely saw their own mother, and in every way considered me their parent. Yet from the day their father and I separated, neither my children nor I have heard from them or seen them, in spite of some minimal attempts on our parts to reach them."

Just as disturbing to the stepparent can be the drama of going to court and posing as good parent material. When a remarried man, for example, tries to modify a custody decree on the grounds that he has a new wife and can now provide a home for his child, the judge will take a good look at the stepmother. Is he or she willing to accept the child as his or her own? Or is the stepparent hostile as the legend suggests? Whether the parent succeeds in the attempt to alter the custody decree depends on how the stepparent performs in court, and one wonders how many women force themselves to muster up a maternal façade in order to help their new husband win his children away from his ex-wife.

I don't mean to overdraw the picture of the helpless stepparent. While weak in law, the stepparent has real powers. A stepfather can persuade his new wife to move to another city or part of the country where the real father will have a hard time visiting his child. Unless the divorce decree specifies that the child shall not be moved (and in the United States, with an increasingly mobile population, courts are more and more reluctant to impose such restrictions), a stepparent has considerable freedom to place himself between the child and his natural parent. Even visiting rights cannot protect a father's interests day in and day out. Speaking of his ex-wife's boy friend, a Seattle businessman said bitterly, "I wish he'd spend time with his own children and leave it to me to entertain my own."

Along with the rise in divorce, there has been a dramatic increase in the number of stepparents who adopt their stepchildren. Whether they should or not is highly controversial. The fact remains that they are doing it. In Britain one-third of all adoptions are by stepfathers. The proportion seems to be even higher in the United States. Statistics from the Department of Health, Education and Welfare show that more children are now adopted by relatives than by strangers and that, at last counting, 46 per cent of these relatives were stepparents. Here is another illustration of the popular amnesia about step-relations and preference for the cosier myths of adoption. When people say "adoption," they mean adoption by stranger even though adoption by relatives has been as common or commoner as the following table shows.

Child adoptions by type (in thousands)						
United States	1952	1960	1965	1968	1970	1971*
Total	85	107	142	166	175	169
By relatives	43	49	65	80	82	86
By non-relatives	42	58	77	86	89	83

Two forces are at work behind these figures. One is the decline in the number of babies available for adoption by childless couples, because of better contraception, changed laws on abortion, and a greater tolerance toward unmarried mothers who want to keep their babies. The other is that stepfathers are increasing among the ranks of adopting relatives because those other relatives who tend to adopt – grandparents, aunts and uncles, older brothers and sisters – have traditionally stepped

* The National Center for Social Statistics has not published recent figures for lack of sufficient data.

in at the loss of a parent through death, and that phenomenon itself is in decline.

In adoption the original parent must surrender his rights. Why would anybody do this? Some men (it is almost always the male parent who is replaced) are happy to be relieved of the obligation to support a child. Others want to cut every tie with the previous marriage. Also, in many cases, the legitimate father cannot be traced, and a court can decide that he has relinquished parental rights by neglect. There are an increasing number of cases in the United States in which courts consent to an adoption over the objection of the noncustodial natural parent.

The case of Arthur Nichol shows the satisfaction that a step-family can find through the process of adoption. For him, adopting his stepdaughters was almost simultaneous with marriage. He was marrying for the first time, his wife for the second, and as part of their prenuptial bargain agreed that he would adopt her two school-aged daughters and that they would have no babies of their own. "We felt that two children were enough." The girls' own father, who lived in the same Mid-western city, did not object. Arthur interpreted the natural father's reasoning:

He thought it appropriate as we were going to be the family unit. It was largely because of the name thing – it can be very embarrassing when the children don't have the same name as their mother and father. The father consented to waiving the waiting period required by state law. We were married in June. I adopted them in November. It was all very exciting for them. They were in kindergarten and first grade. There was no confusion. The older one practiced writing her new name. . . . I noticed the other day that she was writing to her father's mother and she misspelled her old last name.

Anyway, the adoption was a useful step. It symbolized that we were a family unit. My role otherwise would have been too ambiguous. My wife's first husband's parents did not object to the adoption, even though they have no other grandchildren. They were always fond of my wife. They were happy for the children to be in a family again.

The girls' real father hardly sees them at all; sometimes there will be fifteen months between visits. The older girl is worried about loyalties. How is she supposed to feel toward her father? What should she call him?

"They call me Daddy now," Arthur says:

> It grew naturally between us, this confidence. Before we married, Jane and I did not live together, but I baby-sat. Now when we put them to bed, they like to chatter to us. That's when we explain about different kinds of love and how there's not just a limited amount, but that you can love one person fully and still be able to love another person as well. We tell them he loves them in his way. We never say anything against him but we drum it into them, "Think before you get married!"
>
> They miss me a lot when I take business trips. It distresses them, and I try to keep the trips to one day. I postponed one trip because Alice, the oldest, was having her tonsils out.
>
> Stepfatherhood has been a more favorable experience than I anticipated. I am very fortunate. My wife did a magnificent job of getting them started. They are orderly. They are rarely punished; they have a strong sense of rules.

Arthur broke off the conversation to take the temperature of one of the girls who had a sore throat. His wife was out. Both girls came into the living-room in their nightgowns, and one by one – they are getting big and he is a small man – they hopped up on his hip to be carried off to bed. "It is a success story," he acknowledged when he returned. "I know lots of people have trouble with their stepchildren. Why is it so good with us?"

It did look good, although the elder child's doubts may already presage the kind of crisis of identity that adopted children suffer in adolescence when they want to trace their real parents.

The advantages of adopting stepchildren are both legal and psychological. Adoption is permanent, and it gives the stepchild status and rights indistinguishable from any other child of the marriage. For many stepfamilies it spells emotional security. The stepparent need not fear losing the child, and the child's natural anxiety about the stepparent withdrawing affection will be allayed and he will have less need to be jealous of new babies born to the marriage. It ends the haziness of the incest taboos in the stepfamily.

The arguments against are also powerful. They center on the fact that adoption not only creates a new family link, it destroys one. Adoption by stepparent implies that a natural parent has been deprived of his parental rights, and not always voluntarily. There are a number of states with statutes providing that the consent of a parent to adoption is not necessary if he has been deprived of custody in a divorce. Yet losing custody is far less drastic than losing parental rights. The laws have presumably been passed to help stepparents who want to adopt the spouse's child who is living in the home. The assumption is that since the child will be living with the stepparent anyway, his legal rights and obligations should coincide with the family relationship. "Even if this is good social policy," Clark argues, "it is in sharp conflict with ideas of parental right, and it does seem hard on the parent who does not have custody."

In Britain the prevailing view is that to encourage stepparent adoption is bad social policy. The Houghton Committee on adoption law reform in 1972 came down strongly against the practice. The committee's basic argument was that adoption is an irrevocable legal act that cuts a legitimate child off not only from one of its legitimate biological parents but from an entire half of his own family. It wipes out kinship links with brothers, cousins, grandparents, and aunts. For the many stepparents with stepchildren by divorce, the Houghton Committee felt that in most cases guardianship was a better solution. If stepparents were embarrassed by the difference in surname, the name could be legally changed. Any uncertainty about inheritance could be eliminated by providing for the stepchild in a will. With a stepparent as a guardian, a stepchild would retain the option of reverting to his real father's name later in life if he wanted.

Behind these objections lay serious doubts about the motives behind stepchild adoption. The mother may urge adoption as a way of forcing the stepfather to demonstrate his commitment to her and her children. Or the couple together may be trying to take revenge on the ex-husband, by obliterating his tie to the children.

The Houghton Committee's advice was embodied in the Childrens Bill sent to Parliament in 1975. The new law accepts guardianship as the preferred alternative for many stepparents wanting a legal form of relationship with their stepchildren, except that it is now to be called custodianship. It means that the legal custody of the child is transferred to the stepparent, but that the child keeps his original family name and ties.

Stepparent adoption is yet another example of supposedly enlightened attitudes in conflict. One holds that adoption is desirable because it gives the stepchild the nearest approximation to the secure status of a child living with his two natural parents. The other holds that a child's identity is derived from his real kin, that it is his unique biological and cultural inheritance that should not be taken away.

Which is right I would not presume to say. But it does seem sad that stepfamilies get no help – as adoptive parents do – in exploring their attitudes toward these highly emotional issues. Some states are beginning to require that adoptions by a relative go through the same kind of investigation that is mandatory for adoptions by a stranger. The idea is sound, because research has shown that adoptions by relatives can present as many, if not more, emotional problems than adoptions by strangers. If the child is illegitimate, the relative or stepfather who adopts it may be worried about whether the child has inherited a tendency toward promiscuity. There is the immense worry about explaining to the child what happened to the absent parent. An all too common way of dealing with these anxieties is to become a secret stepfather. A British study showed that 50 per cent of adoptive stepparents interviewed had not told the child the truth, a far higher proportion than among other kinds of adoptive couples.

Perhaps counseling stepparents before adoption is a social service that could be undertaken by the hundreds of adoption agencies who now have a dwindling supply of babies to place. They have the trained social workers, the expertise, the financial resources to do the job. What they do lack (unless backed by a law such as Connecticut's) is any authority to interview a stepfamily before an adoption goes through. For what can they do if they find that the stepfather is not a suitable parent for the stepchild? They cannot recommend that the mother divorce her husband and that the child leave the home. Barring flagrant cases of abuse that might be uncovered, the social agencies cannot play God, as they do when placing a baby in a new family, but they can help families to come to terms with the mixed feelings and deep anxieties inherent in the situation. It is not an unimportant use of their skills.

Before deciding to adopt, stepparents should examine their consciences. Do they need the legal status of parents? Do they want their relationship to the child to continue beyond marriage? Are there relatives who might try to claim the child if the natural parent died? Are they ashamed to admit that their spouse has been married before? Are they after revenge or social convenience?

Much that adoption workers have learned over the years can be applied to the benefit of adopting stepparents. Three findings in particular are relevant: 1. children who do not know who their natural parents are suffer in adolescence from a sense of genealogical bewilderment; 2. adoption ends childlessness but not the disappointment over infertility; 3. adoption works best when parents accept the peculiarities of their substitute role, least well when these are denied.

CHAPTER 12

Facing up to remarriage

"Why do we have to have all these arguments?" my stepson asked my husband and me one day when he was about seventeen. "I see other families," he said, "and they just leave each other alone and go their own way and it's like, well, great." His envy of other people's families reminded me of the opening to *Anna Karenina*: "Happy families are all alike. Every unhappy family is unhappy in its own way." It sounds fine, but it is false. What is true is that each family is a family in its own way.

The belief that they deviate from the normal is a burden carried by stepfamilies. It is an unnecessary burden, for the unbroken home is a myth and always has been. There is nothing new about all this changing of spouses (sequential polygamy, the anthropologists call it) and all these stepchildren. Remarriage after widowhood has always been common and quick: "I married another, oh then, oh then." And as an ideal, indissoluble marriage has always been unworkable. All that is new is divorce as a remedy on a large scale. In the past death saved many marriages from reaching the breaking point, but separations, desertions, and adulteries were commonplace. Failing severe social constraints, people have always chosen to live with whom they love. What they did in the past, without divorce, was what they do today in places like Brazil where divorce is not yet permitted. They form illegal stable unions and live in households where a new spouse and the children of a former marriage are thrown together. The stepfamily, a mended broken home, is a normal and traditional family pattern.

Why then has Western society never come to terms with the stepparent? Why have no customs been evolved to ease relations between stepparents and stepchildren? Contemporary society, supposedly analytical, has responded to the increasing number of children involved in divorce by asking a question no more subtle than whether or not divorce encourages juvenile delinquency – and given itself the comforting answer that divorce itself doesn't cause harm, not very much anyway, for children are better off with divorced parents than with a mother and father who are fighting all the time. At the same time, society has become very attentive to the problems of formerly married adults. These are encouraged to find new mates and to gain strength from the trauma of divorce. Meanwhile, the community protects their feelings. Hostesses will take great care not to invite the ex-wife and ex-husband to the same party. But when it comes to the children involved, all are thrown together in school and at play and at camp. No one thinks twice about asking a child to a birthday party where he will meet the child of the woman with whom his own father is now living. Children are supposed not to mind these things.

A society determined to have divorce on demand has not done its homework. Where is the conventional wisdom for getting along with a stepchild? Where are the instructive pamphlets from the Department of Health, Education, and Welfare, "So You're Going to be a Stepfather!"? Where are the mimeographed notices from the Parent-Teachers Association saying that stepfathers are welcome to attend meetings? Where is the social-welfare counseling for the man whose wife is pressing him to adopt her child?

The answer is obvious. The guidance is not there because society cannot face the fact that it has exchanged one unworkable ideal for another. It has given up indissoluble marriage because, like premarital chastity, it was unrealistic. But it has not given up the belief that an unbroken happy home is essential for a child's sound emotional development. To examine the darker feelings inherent in the step-relationship stirs up anxieties that are too strong for the P.T.A. and Parents Without Partners. They may be too strong for social agencies as well. "We have nothing to offer a stepparent," said an experienced social worker, head of a large organization dedicated to helping unmarried mothers. "There are no norms, no standards for stepparenthood," she said. "And if we did meet the man who was going to marry an

unwed mother, which is unlikely – she won't bring him to us –
if we tried to explore with him some of the possible tensions with
the child, we might scare him off."

There may not be norms for successful stepparenthood. But
there are expectations. From what stepparents say about themselves, from gossip, from the press, from stories, from what other
relatives say, I have extracted four.

1. A stepparent must be seen not to be cruel.

2. A stepparent must not try to usurp the place of the natural
parent.

3. A stepparent must supply whatever elements of parenting a
stepchild lacks or the spouse demands.

4. A stepparent must love the stepchild.

It should be obvious that these expectations conflict. They set
a trap into which hundreds of thousands of unsuspecting adults
walk every year. Stepparenthood is a relationship that pits the
myth of the Cruel Stepparent against the Instant Parent, *The
Sound of Music* against *Snow White*, Julie Andrews against the
Wicked Queen. The Instant Parent myth is more ubiquitous than
people realize. You hear it in conversation all the time. It popped
up in the closing scenes of the nostalgic film *The Way We Were*.
Barbra Streisand and Robert Redford have gotten a divorce
because, as has been made blindingly clear, they are politically
and culturally incompatible. They do not divorce, however, until
she has had a baby; then Redford leaves. Some years pass and
Streisand, campaigning for nuclear disarmament, meets Redford
on Central Park South. He has a WASP blonde, in furs, on his
arm. Streisand tells him she has found a good Jewish husband. "Is he a good father?" Redford asks hopefully about his
daughter's stepfather. "He's a *wonderful* father," says Streisand,
emphatically, chin up, and the audience believes it because it is
such a comfortable idea to take home.

How ironic it is that this denial of the tensions of stepparenthood accompanies a social and sexual revolution on behalf of
honesty in personal relationships!

I wonder if the contemporary world is as easy about divorce
as it seems. Some of the ancient guilt about remarriage may
survive from earlier times. The Wife of Bath in *The Canterbury*

Tales is highly defensive about having had five husbands. She lashes out at Saint Jerome's teaching that a marriage should last for eternity, not just for life, and that remarriage is bigamy. The ban against widows taking second husbands was common in prewar India and China and can still be found in quiet corners of the world. Even in our society, the unsophisticated may reveal a sense of guilt about choosing twice. A remarried elderly widow I spoke with always referred to her present husband – of about fifteen years' standing – as Mr. Evans and her first as "my husband." She reflected: "There's nobody like your first husband, is there?" The divorced cannot indulge the superstition that they are still married to the first spouse, but they may harbor it all the same. It was amusing to hear – he even laughed himself – an eminent divorce lawyer mention that he and his wife had concealed from their children for nearly twenty years the fact that she had briefly been married to someone else in her youth. "We didn't actually think of it as a *secret*," he said. "We just didn't mention it. The marriage had been very short, after all, and there were no children. . . . Well, I think that we like to give our children the idea that their parents were each other's only choice."

Children do want their original parents as a unique pair, and they dream, even after a divorce, that their parents will get together again. A children's storybook brought home by my young daughter from the local library told of two identical girls who met at summer camp and realized that they were really twin sisters who had been separated by their parents' divorce. By swapping places when they returned home, the girls were able to make the parents realize how much they missed each other, and to remarry. The story had moved an anonymous child to scrawl on the inside cover, in pencil: "I've just found out a terrible thing. Mom doesn't love us any more." No, children do not like divorce. The late Alexander Onassis, who died in a plane crash in 1973, suffered a shock when his parents divorced in 1960, according to his obituary in the London *Times*. He and his sister Christina, the obituary thought fit to say, "had always entertained hopes for a reunion between their parents, especially after their mother and her second husband were divorced last year," even though, the obituary did not add, their father was not available for remarriage, being then married to the former Mrs. Kennedy.

If the much-married jet set's children cannot accept the reality of divorce and remarriage, it may be a sign that many young people find this an emotional exercise impossible to perform. Research has shown that a surprisingly large percentage of children consider their homes happy or very happy before divorce. So what is to be done about irreconcilables? Children do not like divorce or substitute parents. Adults demand the freedom to live with whom they love.

Face up to the tensions and concentrate on the marriage. It is not a poor choice that society has made to give the ideal of a loving marriage higher priority than that of an unbroken home for children. Remarrying parents have a great asset to offer step-children: the sight of a happy marriage. Statistics suggest that second marriages are stable, that people are likely to remain in them until they are broken by death. To many people, their happiness justifies the pain they have caused their children, for they believe, although they do not say so outright, that it is an adult's world. Their children will have their turn in time. The parents are proud of their passions. They have had the courage to insist on genuine love in their own lives, and this is the goal that they want their children to aim for. A doctor told me about the misery his divorce had inflicted on his children: "It was the most wrenching thing I have ever done." Then he went on to say: "My remarriage was a renaissance for me. I have grown professionally and intellectually. It has been beneficial to the children too, I think. They see a marriage working. They know it is actively sexual. It gives them hope."

There is no formula for eliminating the strains between step-parent and stepchild, but more honesty and less pretending can only help. Both adult and child should be kept free from the expectation that they love each other, that they act as parent and child. If love grows, well and good. If not, fine, too. All that should be demanded on both sides is politeness. The special tensions of the family then need to be recognized. Husband and wife should between themselves consider the implications of the absence of the incest taboo in their particular household. All

questions of money, allowances, and inheritances should be
sorted out before the wedding. (Some older couples enter into
prenuptial agreements to ensure that their respective children
will inherit their estate intact.) Then, when stepfamily life gets
going, the children themselves should be drawn into consultation. What are the differences in operating as a stepfamily, not as
a biological family? What face should they put to the world?
How do they want to be introduced? What should they all call
each other? Some sociologists go so far as to say that the stepfamily is as structurally and pyschologically different from the
nuclear family as is the Israeli kibbutz. What do teen-age children
think?

Comparisons with other families being inevitable, stepfamilies
should learn where the true comparisons lie. Not with mothers
and fathers, but with new babies and with parents-in-law. In-
truders, rivals, one generation with interests in conflict with
another. If there is anything "natural" in the step-relationship,
it is the element of rivalry. We have come to live with the fact
that not only children but even *fathers* are jealous of new babies.
That stepparents and stepchildren resent each other is not so
ugly a thought that it needs to be left hidden.

I think attempts to abolish the *step-* terms are ridiculous. They
stem from the faith in positive thinking that has produced such
absurdities as "mental health" and "chairperson." If the con-
notation is unpleasant, the reason should be faced, not glossed
over with a change of label. If new terminology is wanted –
realistic, not euphemistic – why not "by marriage"? I am a
mother-by-marriage: this is my daughter-by-marriage. It is a
description of the affinal tie that is accurate and has a nice upbeat
sound. It harks back to the old (also legally accurate) "mother-in-
lawe," and what is more, it implies breakability. This is my
grandfather-by-marriage, for as long as that marriage lasts.

If the *step-* terms were used more openly, the step-relationship
could come out from under cover. Stepparents would be visible
in their millions. It may be impracticable for censuses to count
stepfathers, but there are informal ways that the status might
be recognized and a social role defined. Schools could help a lot.
They could begin by facing the fact that class lists, with the

child's name and home address, are not used only to find out
where to send invitations to birthday parties. They are used
to establish the child's identity. To put Sandra Brown, daughter
of Mrs. Joseph Watson, 100 Memorial Drive, usually serves to
tell everybody that Mrs. Watson has divorced and remarried and
deprives Mr. Brown of his right to public identification as the
child's father. Such public listing of a child's name should, I
think, be followed by the full names and addresses of both living
parents and the stepparent should be identified as a stepparent.
Schools should routinely expect four parents per child on social
occasions, and principals and teachers should acknowledge the
remarried. "We are happy to welcome so many parents and stepparents here today." Why not Stepfathers' Day? Why not greeting cards for stepparents? This is not a frivolous suggestion. I
used to work for a greeting card publisher and was interested to
learn of the narrow slices of the population that warranted cards
of their own. "On the Anniversary of your Ordination" was a
strong seller; get-well cards for the dying were another. I will
leave it to those still in the trade to devise the cute verses and
artwork that could go "To a Stepmother on her Birthday."

The ambiguous stepfather needs assistance. There have been
radical suggestions as to what form it might take. Certain sociologists, social-work reformers, and women's liberationists say:
dethrone fatherhood. Let society recognize the mother-child
pair as the basic family unit, force the state to accept responsibility
for supporting them, and let women have husbands as they
choose. The counterargument is that such a reform could not
take place without throwing out the principle of legitimacy on
which present laws and customs are based. What this principle
means is that society recognizes the group of mother and child
to be incomplete without a father and that he – a single, identifiable male – is the source of the child's status in the community.

It seems to me that there may be a solution short of full con-
version to matriarchy. Fatherhood, vague as it is, has always had
two aspects – biological and sociological. A stepfather could be
allowed to assume some of the sociological functions of a male
parent around the house without infringing on the legitimate

father's rights. Stepfathers could be encouraged to teach their stepchildren skills, and they could be pressed into service in helping the children make the transition into the adult world. If they were allowed to have sex-linked duties toward the child, as stepmothers have, they would feel less like third wheels and perhaps press less fiercely for parental rights.

At the same time, fair's fair. Stepfathers should not be asked to assume the financial burdens of a runaway husband who has managed to get lost. Fathers should be protected better than they are upon divorce. Children should not be allowed to be adopted against the father's protests, except in very special circumstances. There should be a general acceptance of two last names within a family. Mailboxes should read Smith and Jones. A society that wants nearly a million divorces a year cannot afford to be embarrassed when the children in a household don't have the same surname as their father and mother. Like millions of other children, they have their father's name and their mother has remarried. What is difficult about that?

A remarrying society needs to get rid of a lot of archaic ideas. One is that the woman has some obligation to perform domestic work for her husband and for her husband's children when they turn up. Another is the idea that divorce totally severs a marriage. Some enlightened people (enlightened usually by expensive lawyers) arrange arbitration procedures when they divorce in order to resolve, without reopening old wounds, the inevitable decisions and conflicts of opinion that arise over the children of the marriage as time goes by. A third illusion that should go is that psychotherapy can ignore the extraordinary circumstances of the step-relation and focus only on The Child.

I think I can answer my stepson's question now. Why did we have all those arguments? Because we pretended. We masqueraded as a nuclear family and we were not. And we let ourselves imagine that unbroken homes are happier than they are.

There are a few plain truths about stepparenthood that I learned writing this book. I was blind not to have recognized them when I got married. Stepfamilies can be happy, even happier than families in which there has never been more than one mother or father but it takes more work. The tensions of the stepfamily are special and real. A stepparent *cannot* be the same as a real parent. There are no new Mommies and new Daddies. Yet there are compensations for the strains. My own particular reward has been to help two young people who are nothing like me to be more like themselves and to watch the bond grow between the two sets of children. Stepfamilies in general do have positive advantages. When a stranger has to be taken into the family circle, when children have a parent who lives somewhere else, the family has an extra dimension. There is not that claustrophobia that led the anthropologist Dr. Edmund Leach to describe the ordinary family "with its narrow privacy and tawdry secrets" as "the source of all our discontents." The stepfamily is open and tough. It is not a bad place to live, for those who can accept the uncomfortable fact that many of the tensions between stepparents and stepchildren will be inevitable as long as spouses are replaceable and parents are not.

Notes

Paul Bohannan, *International Encyclopedia of Social Sciences,* Vol. 10, "Marriage," ed. D. Sills. (London, The Macmillan Co. and the Free Press, 1968.)

Robin Fox, *Kinship and Marriage.* (London, Penguin, 1967.)

24 F. L. Lucas, *Greek Drama for the Common Reader.* (London, Chatto and Windus, 1967.)

29 Bronislaw Malinowski, "Parenthood: The Basis of Social Structure," in *The Family: Its Structure and Its Functions,* ed. R. I. Coser. (New York, St. Martin's Press, 1964), p. 6.

29 Talcott Parsons, "The Kinship System of the Contemporary United States," in *Essays in Sociological Theory,* Revised Edition. (New York, Free Press, 1964), p. 187.

30 E. N. Goody, "Forms of Pro-Parenthood: The Sharing and Substitution of Parental Roles," in *Kinship,* ed. J. Goody. (London, Penguin Books, 1971.)

31 Margaret Mead, "Anomalies in American Postdivorce Relationships," in *Divorce and After,* ed. Paul Bohannan. (New York, Anchor Books, 1971.)

CHAPTER 3

32 Jessie Bernard, *Remarriage.* (New York, Russell and Russell, 1971.)

32 Edward Podolsky, "The emotional problems of the stepchild," *Mental Hygiene,* 1955, *39,* pp. 49–53.

34 British Association of Adoption Agencies, "Explaining Adoption," London, 1972.

34 Homer F. Clark, *Law of Domestic Relations.* (St. Paul, Minn., West, 1968.)

34 Definitions of step-relations:

Random House Dictionary of the English Language: stepmother: a woman who occupies one's mother's place by marriage to one's father.

The Shorter Oxford English Dictionary: stepmother: the wife of one's father by a subsequent marriage.

Webster's Third New International Dictionary of the English Language Unabridged: stepmother: the wife of one's father by a subsequent marriage.

(However: the 12-volume *New Oxford English Dictionary* defines stepmother as "a woman who has married one's father after one's mother's death" clearly associating the "step" prefix with the death of a parent. It describes the "step" prefix as designating the degrees of affinity resulting from the remarriage of a widowed parent.)

Nouveau Larousse Universel: belle-mère: Mère du mari ou de la femme. Par rapport aux enfants, celle qui a épousé leur frère.

34-5 *New Oxford English Dictionary:* mother-in-law: 1. The mother of one's husband or wife. 2. Stepmother. Examples from Henry Fielding's *Miser*, 1732 and Vives' *Instruction for Christian Women, 1540.* Second usage now regarded as incorrect.

35 The Brothers Grimm, *Grimms' Fairy Tales.* (New York, Grosset & Dunlap, 1963.)

35 Alan Macfarlane, *The Family Life of Ralph Josselin: A Seventeenth Century Clergyman.* (London, Cambridge University Press, 1970.)

36 John C. Fitzpatrick, ed., *Writings of Washington.* Washington D.C., U.S. Government Printing Office, Vol. 2, 1925.

36 Marcus Cunliffe, *George Washington, Man and Monument.* (London, Collins, 1959.)

36 George Eliot, *Daniel Deronda.* (New York, Dutton, 1964.)

36 Ovid, *Metamorphoses,* Book One, l. 149.

37 Dr. Benjamin Spock, *Problems of Parents.* (New York, Curtis, 1955.)

37 Paul Bohannan, ed., *Divorce and After.* (New York, Doubleday, 1971), p. 135.

38 Jack Goody, "On Nannas and Nannies," *Man,* December 1962.

38 Gospel According to St. Luke, ii, 48, 49.

40 Spock, *Problems of Parents.*

41 *The Times,* Law Report, July 31, 1973.

42 William Shakespeare, *Cymbeline,* Act I, Scene i.

43 William Shakespeare, *Hamlet,* Act I, Scene ii.

43 Fitzpatrick, *Writings of Washington, op. cit.,* Vol. 3.

CHAPTER 4

46 William Goode, *World Revolution and Family Patterns.* (New York, Free Press, 1963.)

49 Robert Lucas, *Frieda Lawrence.* (London, Secker and Warburg, 1973.)

49 Lucas, *ibid.*

50 Maria von Trapp, *Maria*. (London, Creation House, 1972.)

52 D. H. Lawrence, *The Rainbow*. (London, Penguin, 1949.)

52 Goode, *World Revolution*.

53 Carl Sandburg, *Abraham Lincoln*, Vol. 1 "The Prairie Years." (New York, Harcourt Brace, 1926.)

54 D. C. Disney, "Second Marriage: The Daughters Couldn't Get Along," *Ladies' Home Journal*, August 1967.

58 Margot Asquith, *The Autobiography of Margot Asquith*, Vol. 1. (London, Thornton Butterworth, 1920.)

59 The Duchess of Bedford related this anecdote in a B.B.C. television interview "The Bedfords' Goodbye to Woburn," quoted in *The Listener*, April 18, 1974.

60-1 Norman Mailer, *Prisoner of Sex*. (Boston, Mass., Little, Brown and Company, 1971.)

62 *Hamlet*, Act III, Scene iv, l. 68-69.

62 Lawrence, *The Rainbow*.

63 Emily Post, *Etiquette*. (New York, Funk and Wagnalls, 1922.)

CHAPTER 5

65 C. E. Bowerman and D. P. Irish, "Some Relationships of Stepchildren to their Parents," *Marriage and Family Living*, 1962, *24*, pp. 113-121.

66 Irene Fast and Albert Cain, "The Stepparent Role, Potential for Disturbances in Family Functioning," *American Journal of Orthopsychiatry*, 1966, *36*, pp. 485-491.

66 William C. Smith, *The Stepchild*. (Chicago, University of Chicago Press, 1953.)

66 Annie White, "Factors Making for Difficulty in the Stepparent Relationship with Children," Illinois Institute for Juvenile Research, 1943, abstract of thesis.

66 N. Khalique, "A Study of Insecurity Feeling and Anxiety in Stepchildren and Non-Stepchildren," *Journal of Psychological Research*, Madras, 1961, *5*, pp. 114-115.

67 Edward Podolsky, "Emotional Problems of the Stepchild," *Mental Hygiene*, 1955, *39*, pp. 49-53.

67 Gerda Schulman, "Myths that Intrude on the Adaptation of the Stepfamily," *Social Casework*, 1972, *53*, pp. 131-139.

67 Lucille Duberman, "Stepkin Relationships," *Journal of Marriage and the Family*, May 1973, pp. 283-292.

69 Else P. Heilpern, "Psychological Problems of Stepchildren," *Psychoanalytic Review*, 1943, *30*, pp. 163–176.

70 J. C. Fluegel, *The Psychoanalytic Study of the Family*. (London, Hogarth Press, 1931.)

71 Otto Rank, *The Myth of the Birth of the Hero*. (New York, Nervous and Mental Diseases Pub., 1914.)

71 Edward Conklin, "The Foster-Child Fantasy," *American Journal of Psychology*, 1920, *31*, pp. 59 ff.

71 Sigmund Freud, "Mourning and Melancholia," *Collected Papers*, Vol. IV. (London, Hogarth Press, 1924.)

71 Helen Deutsch, "Absence of Grief," *The Psychoanalytic Quarterly*, 1937, *6*, pp. 12–21.

72 Gilbert Kliman *et al.*, "Facilitation of Mourning During Childhood," The Center for Preventive Psychiatry, White Plains, New York, 1973.

73 Bowerman and Irish's paper (*op. cit.*) presents a clear review of the evidence on stepchildren's reactions to death and divorce.

74 Duberman, "Stepkin Relationships."

76 Nancy Mitford, *The Pursuit of Love*. (London, Hamish Hamilton, 1945.)

76–7 Newspaper reports of stepchildren breaking up marriages can be found in the *Chicago Tribune*, June 5, 1974 ("This route to parenthood goes a step beyond" by Linda Lee Landis) and the *Boston Sunday Globe*, October 14, 1973 ("The blended family – a byproduct of divorce" by Bill Fripp).

CHAPTER 6

83–4 Anthony Burgess, "Thoughts of a Belated Father," *The Spectator*, September 6, 1968.

85 Asquith, *Autobiography*.

87 Leo Tolstoy, *Anna Karenina*, 1901.

88 Sigmund Freud, *Totem and Taboo*. (London, Routledge Paperback, 1960.)

88 *Writings of Washington*. Letter to Reverend Jonathan Boucher from Mount Vernon, May 13, 1770.

CHAPTER 7

91 Vladimir Nabokov, *Lolita*. (Paris, Olympia, 1955.)

91 *Sunday Express*, London, September 28, 1974.

91 Fieugel, *Psychoanalytic Study of the Family.*

92 Diane Baroni, "Weekend Stepmother," *Cosmopolitan* (U.S. edition), April 1974.

92 Meade, "Anomalies in American Post-Divorce Relationships."

93 Leonore C. Terr, "A Family Study in Child Abuse," *American Journal of Psychiatry*, November 1970.

96 Schulman, "Myths that Intrude on the Stepfamily."

96 Heilpern, "Psychological Problems of Stepchildren."

96 Nabokov, *Lolita.*

96 Carter and Glick, *Marriage and Divorce.*

96 Giuseppe Verdi, *Don Carlo*, 1867.

96 Eugene O'Neill, *Desire Under the Elms*, 1924.

97 Geoffrey Chaucer, "The Merchant's Tale," *The Poetical Works of Chaucer*, ed. F. N. Robinson. (Boston, Houghton Miflin, 1933.)

97 Nabokov, *Lolita.*

97 Jean Racine, *Phèdre and Other Plays*, trans. by John Cairncross. (London, Penguin, 1963.)

99 H. K. Bevan, *The Law Relating to Children.* (London, Butterworths, 1973.)

99 Herbert Maisch, *Incest.* (London, André Deutsch, 1973.)

100 Caleb Foote *et al.*, *Cases and Materials on Family Law.* (Boston, Little Brown, 1966.)

100 American Humane Association, *Child Victims of Incest*, Denver, Colorado, 1963.

100 A. L. Kroeber, "Stepdaughter Marriage," *American Anthropologist*, N.S. 42, 1940.

101 Irvine Kaufman *et al.*, "The Family Constellation and Overt Incestuous Relations Between Father and Daughter," *American Journal of Orthopsychiatry*, 1954, *24*, p. 266.

102 Maisch, *Incest.*

102 Maisch, *ibid.*

102–4 Emile Durkheim, *Incest, the Nature and Origin of the Taboo.* (New York, Lyle Stuart, 1898.)

102–4 Freud, *Totem and Taboo, op. cit.*

102–4 *International Encyclopedia of Social Science* (Incest entry by Margaret Mead, Vol. 5).

102–4 E. Westermarck, *The History of Human Marriage.* (London, 1891.)

102–4 Leslie A. White, "The Definition and Prohibition of Incest," *American Anthropologist*, N.S. 50, 1948.

102-4 Talcott Parsons, "The Incest Taboo in Relation to the Social Structure and the Socialization of the Child," *British Journal of Sociology*, 1954, 5.

104 *King James Bible*, Leviticus, 18:8, 18:17.

104 *Catholic Encyclopedia*, Church of England's Tables of Kindred and Affinity, *Encyclopedia Judaica*.

105 Shakespeare, *Hamlet*, Act I, Scene ii.

105 W. S. Gilbert and Arthur Sullivan, *Iolanthe*, 1882.

105 Clark, *On Domestic Relations*.

108 Clark quotes Henderson v. State, 26 Ala. App. 263, 157 So. 884 (1934) in which the court held that where there were no children of the marriage, the stepmother's relation by affinity to her stepson ended on the death of the stepson's father, so that the marriage of the stepmother with the stepson did not violate Alabama's incest statute.

108 American Bar Association, 4 *Family Law Quarterly*, 209, Sept. 1970.

108 Nabokov, *Lolita*.

109 Racine, *Phèdre*.

109 Clark, *On Domestic Relations*.

CHAPTER 8

111 Census Bureau report, "Fertility Histories."

111 Census Bureau report, Series P-20, No. 239, "Marriage, Divorce and Remarriage by Year of Birth," June 1971, Tables D and G.

112 Census Bureau informal report, "Recent Trends and Variations in Marriage and the Family," November 1973.

112 Claude Levi-Strauss, *The Elementary Structures of Kinship*. (Boston, Beacon, 1969.)

114 Patience Lauriat, "The Effect of Marital Dissolution," *Journal of Marriage and the Family*, August 1969.

114 Edward Pohlman, "Childlessness, Intentional and Unintentional," *Journal of Nervous and Mental Diseases*, July 1970.

118 President Ford's biography, U.S. Information Service and news reports, August 9, 1974.

119 Sidney Howard, "They knew what they wanted," *Famous American Plays of the 1920s*, ed. Kenneth Macgowan. (New York, Dell, 1959.)

120 Leslie Caron, interview in *Cosmopolitan* (British edition), April 1974.

122 D. C. Disney, "Susan and Chuck were Bachelors," *Ladies' Home Journal*, August 1968.

122 D. C. Disney, "My stepdaughter was a nemesis," *Ladies' Home Journal*, July 1968.

122 D. C. Disney, "Myra had Stepdaughter Trouble," *Ladies' Home Journal*, December 1968.

122 Duberman, "Stepkin Relationships."

CHAPTER 9

123 Charlotte Brontë, *Jane Eyre*, 1847.

126 Paul Bohannan, "Divorce Chains, Households of Remarriage and Multiple Divorces," *Divorce and After*.

126 Jean Baer, *The Second Wife*. (New York, Doubleday, 1972.)

126 Freud, *Totem and Taboo*.

128 Metropolitan Life Insurance Company, New York. *Metropolitan Statistical Bulletin*, September 1972.

128 Peter Laslett, "Parental Deprivation in the Past. A note on the history of orphans in England," *Local Population Studies*, 1974.

128 Peter Laslett, *The World We Have Lost*. (New York, Charles Scribner's and Sons, 1965.)

129 D. C. Disney, "Second Marriage: Their Daughters Couldn't Get Along," *Ladies' Home Journal*, August 1967.

133 Schulman, "Myths that Intrude on the Adaptation of the Stepfamily."

134-5 Schulman, *ibid*.

CHAPTER 10

140 R. Brimley Johnson, ed., *A Book of British Ballads*. (London, Dent, 1966.)

140 Hedrick Smith, "Solzhenitsyn: How They Persecute You," *The Observer*, October 8, 1972.

140-1 Helene Deutsch, *The Psychology of Women*, Vol. II. (London, Research Books, 1947.)

143 Smith, *The Stepchild*.

143 Goode, *World Revolution*.

144   Eudora Welty, *The Optimist's Daughter*. (New York, Random House, 1972.)

146-7 Marian Roalfe Cox, *Cinderella: Three Hundred Forty-Five Variants*. (London, Folk-lore Society, 1893.)

146   Rank, *Myth of the Birth of the Hero*.

146   Franz Ricklin, *Wish Fulfillment and Symbolism in Fairy Tales*. (New York, Nervous and Mental Diseases Pub., 1915.)

148   Donald Marcus, "The Cinderella Motif: Fairy Tale and Defence," *American Imago*, 1963, *20*, p. 1.

148   Fern Marja Eckman, *The Furious Passage of James Baldwin*. (New York, M. Evans and Company, 1966.)

148   Charles Dickens, *David Copperfield*, 1849-50.

148-9 *Grimm's Fairy Tales, op. cit.*

150   George Homans, *English Villagers of the Thirteenth Century*. (New York, Harper Torchbook, 1970.)

150   Lawrence Stone, *Crisis of the Aristocracy, 1558-1641*. (New York, Oxford University Press, 1967.)

151   Anon. "Hunting for a Diana," *Time*, April 2, 1973.

151   Norman Zierold, *The Child Stars*. (New York, Coward-McCann, 1965.)

151   David Gil, *Violence Against Children*. (Cambridge, Mass., Harvard University Press, 1970.)

151   P. D. Scott, "Fatal Battered Baby Cases," *Medical Science and the Law*, 1973, *13*, No. 3.

152   Anon. "I was her mum – I loved her," *The Guardian*, December 1, 1973.

157   Baroni, "Weekend Stepmother."

159   Henry James, *What Maisie Knew*, 1897.

159   Daphne du Maurier, *Rebecca*. (London, Gollancz, 1939.)

160   Georgia Lee Cox, "Confessions of a Wicked Stepmother," *Ladies' Home Journal*, March 1971.

CHAPTER II

163   Nabokov, *Lolita*.

163   The legal background for this chapter was provided by advisers in the United States and Britain, supplemented by Clark's *Domestic Relations* and Bevan's *Law Relating to Children*, both cited previously.

164   Clark cites Root v. Allen, 151 Colo. 311, 377 P.2d 117 (1962),

73 Yale L.J. 151 (1963) and Petition of Hohmann, 255 Minn. 165, 95 N.W. 28643 (1959).

165 Child Action Poverty Group. "As Man and Wife?" London, July 1973.

167 *Statistical Abstract of the United States, 1973*; No. 508, "Child Adoptions by Type," 1952 to 1971.

170 Report of the Departmental Committee on the Adoption of Children. (Houghton Committee.) Her Majesty's Stationery Office. Command paper 5107.

171 Iris Goodacre, *Adoption Policy and Practice*. (London, Allen and Unwin, 1966.)

172 Michael Humphrey, *The Hostage Seekers*. (London, Longmans, 1969.)

172 H. J. Sants, "Genealogical Bewilderment in Children with Substitute Parents." (London, National Council for the Unmarried Mother and her Child, 1966.)

CHAPTER 12

173 Tolstoy, *Anna Karenina*.

176 Erich Kästner, *Lottie and Lisa*. (London, Cape, 1950.)

176 Obituary of Alexander Onassis. *The Times*, January 24, 1973.

177 Paul C. Glick and Arthur J. Norton, "Frequency, Duration and Probability of Marriage and Divorce," *Journal of Marriage and the Family*, May 1971.

178 Fast and Cain, previously cited, compared the stepfamily to the kibbutz in its structural difference from ordinary family life.

181 Edmund Leach, *A Runaway World?* Reith Lectures 1967. (London, B.B.C., 1968.)

Index